Advance praise for _The Episco_

"When Episcopal educators ha⸱ person we turn to is Sharon Ely Pearson. Fortunately for us, Sharon has compiled answers to her most frequently asked questions in this informative, readable and even humorous gem of a book. Whether we are brand-new to this work or have years of experience under our belts, _The Episcopal Christian Educator's Handbook_ is for us. Just reading the Table of Contents is worth the price. It's everything we need to know, right at our fingertips."

—_Barbara Tensen Ross_
Missioner for Lifelong Christian Formation,
The Episcopal Diocese of Oregon

"Theological and practical, biblical and humorous, _The Episcopal Christian Educator's Handbook_ is a treasure trove of wisdom, information, and guidance garnered from Sharon Pearson's vast experience as a highly regarded leader in this field and geared to the specific context of The Episcopal Church. The well-organized volume covers everything from a discussion of the nature of Christian Formation, to tips about where to put the First Aid Kit, to how to maintain sanity in this vocation. This is a comprehensive, accessible, delightful resource that novice and experienced educators alike will want to have on their bookshelves. What a gift!"

—_The Rev. Canon Patricia S. Mitchell_
Canon for Christian Formation, The Episcopal Diocese of New York

"_The Episcopal Christian Educator's Handbook_ is a nice, concise collection of information suitable for those new to the ministry of Christian education and formation. The mostly one-page entries helpfully explain 'the basics' of Christian education in The Episcopal Church in a readable, light format. This book is particularly suitable for volunteer teachers, DCEs, youth directors, clergy, and vestry members responsible for Christian education in their parishes."

—_Cindy Coe_
Formation Consultant, Episcopal Relief & Development

"_The Episcopal Christian Educator's Handbook_ is a compilation of information and examples, grounded in theology and history. It's your perfect how-to book for children's and youth ministry and would be relevant for both clergy and lay leaders. It's a book that you can hand to those setting up new ministries, or you can hand it to seasoned veterans who wish to learn new concepts or find needed validation in those things they may already know. As a professional consultant to parishes for children and youth ministry, I read many books on this subject, but what sets this book apart is that it provides a sound foundation for Christian formation, from job descriptions to sample teacher's meetings, from ways we understand curriculum theologically to how and why we welcome children into church. This book gives the basics backed by the theory and theology. What a great resource!"

—*Genevieve Callard*
Assistant to the Bishop for Children, Youth, and Young Adult Ministries
The Episcopal Diocese of Western Michigan

"*The Episcopal Christian Educator's Handbook* is a delightfully entertaining collection of practical information, truly 'everything you ever need to know.' Sharon Ely Pearson has created a well-written and thoughtfully organized guide to the job and the ministry of the Christian Educator."

—*Lisa Puccio*
Minister for Children and Families, Christ Church Cathedral,
Houston, Texas, and Vice-President of Forma

"This book is a true gift to Christian educators! It is a 'must have' on the bookshelf and one that should be given to any person who accepts such a position. I wish this had been available years ago when I first took a church position. I would have kept it with me at all times! I look forward to sharing this gift with those in my diocese."

—*Kathy Graham*
Coordinator of Lifelong Christian Formation
The Episcopal Diocese of Alabama and Forma Board member

"Wonderful, extraordinary, honest . . . these are only three words that describe *The Episcopal Christian Educator's Handbook*. Pearson is recognized as one of the top experts in the education/formation field and this book is evidence why. In *The Episcopal Christian Educator's Handbook* she provides a range of information from age-old practical advice, the depth of understanding Lifelong Faith Formation in the twenty-first century, and the congregation's role. She includes contemporary issues such as how to handle new challenges like bullying. For experienced educators it reminds us of the basics we have forgotten. For the new educator it will give you the confidence you will need to excel. This is a must have for all clergy and every seminary student would be wise to read it before their first assignment."

—*Ruth-Ann Collins*
Officer, Lifelong Christian Formation, The Episcopal Church

The Episcopal Christian Educator's Handbook

compiled and edited by Sharon Ely Pearson

Morehouse Publishing
NEW YORK · HARRISBURG · DENVER

With thanks to these individuals who gave permission to share their stories and content: Kim McPherson, Christina Clark, Becky Hudspeth, Maureen Hagan, Sheryl Kujawa-Holbrook, and Keith Anderson.

Part of this book was originally published as *The Lutheran Handbook* © 2005, Augsburg Fortress, and as *The Episcopal Handbook* © 2008 Church Publishing Incorporated.

Unless otherwise noted, the Scripture quotations contained herein are from the New Revised Standard Version Bible, copyright © 1989 by the Division of Christian Education of the National Council of Churches of Christ in the U.S.A. Used by permission. All rights reserved.

"A Sandwich Evaluation" by Delia Halverson is from *How to Train Volunteer Teachers* © 1991 Abingdon Press. Used by permission. All rights reserved.

Morehouse Publishing, 4785 Linglestown Road, Suite 101, Harrisburg, PA 17112

Morehouse Publishing, 19 East 34th Street, New York, NY 10016

Morehouse Publishing is an imprint of Church Publishing Incorporated. www.churchpublishing.org

Cover design by Laurie Klein Westhafer
Typeset by Rose Design
Interior illustrations by Brenda Brown and Dorothy Thompson Perez

Library of Congress Cataloging-in-Publication Data

A catalog record of this book is available from the Library of Congress.

ISBN 13: 978-0-8192-2881-9 (pbk.)
ISBN 13: 978-0-8192-2882-6 (ebook)

Printed in Canada

CONTENTS

Introduction   xi

Christian Ed Stuff   1

What Is Christian Formation?   2

Spiritual Formation vs. Education   3

What Is a Christian Educator?   4

The Call to Be a Christian Educator   5

Director of Christian Education   6

Director of Youth Ministries   8

You've Got the Job!   10

New Girl (or Guy) in Town   11

The 911   12

How to Create a Dream Team   13

Many Parts, but One Body   14

But We *Always* Had Sunday School!   15

Needs vs. Wants   16

Explicit and Implicit   18

What Is *The* Curriculum?   19

Types of Curriculum   20

How to Plan the Year   21

The Church School Teacher   22

Rethinking Recruitment   23

How to Call Volunteers   24

How to Nurture Those in the Trenches   26

We Need S'more Teachers   27

How to Evaluate a Resource   28

How to Assess Your Space   29

How to Assess Your Equipment   31

How to Manage a Crowd   32

A Successful Teachers' (or Any) Meeting   33

Agenda: Formation Style   34

The Two-Adult Rule   35

Why Background Checks?   36

The Church Nursery   37

Fee or Free?   39

Don't Hide It Under a Bushel   40

When's a Youth Not a Youth?   41

What Do You Mean, "Cradle to Grave"?   42

How is Stewardship Formational?   43

How to Include Service and Mission   44

Tourist, Missionary, or Pilgrim?   45

Soccer, Band, Hockey, and the Debate Team   46

How to Be Best Friends with the Altar Guild   47

How to Welcome Children in Worship   48

How to Give a Children's Sermon   49

When the Acolyte's Hair Catches Fire   50

How to Lead Children's Chapel   51

How to Build Faith at Home   52

How to Covet Dedicated Space   53

The "Classroom" of the Future   54

How to Use Technology   55

"Whatcha Gonna Do When They Come for You?"   56

The Three-Legged Stool of Evaluation   57

Teaching Tips   59

How to Have a Successful Class   60

How to Tell *The* Story   61

Johnny's On the Ceiling   62

When Snakes Show Up   63

How We Learn   64

The Brain Created by God   65

An Inclusive Classroom   66

Who Am I? A Preschooler!   67

Who Am I? I'm Six Going on Eight 68

Who Am I? I'm the Big Kid 69

Who Am I? I Really Don't Know 70

Who Am I? I'm Working on It 71

A Roomful of Homer Simpsons 72

Noah Gathered Them Two by Two 73

Prayers To and For Children 74

What to Say When Grandma or Fido Dies 75

How to Get Paint Out of an Easter Dress 76

What Should Be in Your Classroom? 77

How to Minister to Bullies 78

How to Lead Quick Games 80

I Have to Lead an Adult Study? 81

What Adults Should Be Talking About 82

Partiers, Bible Thumpers, or Do-Gooders? 83

Is *This* the Right Question? 84

How to Lead a Book Discussion Group 86

Derailments and Dominators 87

Paperwork and Checklists 89

An Invitation to Serve 90

A Covenant with Teachers and Leaders 91

Recipe for a Church School Lesson 92

Lesson Plan Template 94

The Supply Closet 95

Checklist of Necessary Nursery Supplies 97

An Emergency Plan 98

Where to Put the First Aid Kit 99

A Sandwich Evaluation 100

Curriculum Evaluation Worksheet 101

How to Get Input from Teachers 102

How to Get Input from Parents 103

Registration Forms 104

The Dreaded Permission Slip 105

Media Release   106
A Covenant for a Mission Trip   107
The Budget   108
The Annual Report   109
Prayers to Begin Meetings or the Consumption of Food   110

Episcopal Stuff   111

What Is the Episcopal Church?   112
What Is the Anglican Communion?   113
Provinces of the Episcopal Church   114
How to Use Three-Legged Stools   116
What is the Book of Common Prayer?   117
How Many Hymnals *Are* There?   118
Popular Hymns for Children   119
What is the Lectionary?   120
Days and Seasons of the Church Year   121
How to Teach about Sacraments   126
Sprinkling, Pouring, or Immersion?   127
Holy Communion, Mass, or Eucharist?   129
What *Are* We Confirming?   130
How to Make a Secret Signal   132
What to Do When the Bishop Shows Up   133
Do Episcopalians Believe in Saints?   134
Fifteen Famous Episcopal Christian Educators   135

Your Sanity   139

Stress? What Stress?   140
How to Take Care of Yourself   141
Time Bandits   142
Two Heads are Better Than One   143
How *Not* to Work for Free   144
How to Be the Real Boss: Pray   145
How to Locate Toilet Paper   146
How to Untangle the Triangle   147

E-mail Complaints   148
Spiritual Direction   149
How to Forgive Someone   150
How to Choose the Right Virgin Mary   151
How to Console Others   152
How to Cope with Grief and Loss   153
How to Bless a Child (or Anyone Else)   154
How to Draw the Line   156
How to Avoid Easter Egg Catastrophes   157

Bible Stuff   **159**

Who Wrote the Bible?   160
A Guide to Popular Bible Translations   162
How to Choose a Bible   164
How to Present a Bible   165
How Episcopalians Read the Bible (and Why More Should) 167
But No One Shows Up for Bible Study!   169
The Seven Funniest Bible Stories   170
The Top 10 Bible Miracles (and What They Mean)   173
Four Inspiring Women of the Bible   175
Called Up to the Majors (Prophets, That Is)   176
The Top 10 Bible Villains   178
The Top 10 Bible Heroes   181
Five Gross Bible Stories for Boys (and Girls)   183
Jesus' Fourteen Apostles   184
The Three Most Rebellious Things Jesus Did   186

Maps, Diagrams, and Charts   **187**

The Exodus   188
The Ark of the Covenant   189
Jerusalem in Jesus' Time   190
The Passion and Crucifixion   191
Family Tree of Christianity   198

EpiscoSpeak   **199**

Extra Important Stuff   205

The Lord's Prayer   206
The Ten Commandments   207
The Baptismal Covenant   208
An Outline of the Faith   210
A Children's Charter for the Church   226
The Charter for Lifelong Christian Formation   228
The Five Marks of Mission   230
What Are the Millennium Development Goals?   231
Daily Devotions for Individuals and Families   232
Compline   236
Must-Haves for the Christian Educator's Shelf   244

INTRODUCTION

I've been an Episcopalian all my life and a Christian educator for 70 percent of those years. Whenever I think I've seen it all in ministering with children, youth, or adults I'm thrown a curveball and have to think on my feet. When I first started out, I made it up as I went along, through trial and error as well as depending on some great role models and mentors. I read every "handbook" I could put my hands on and whenever possible attended workshops or conferences. In the beginning that wasn't so easy—I was a volunteer with little time and money, not to mention an infant and a three-year-old in tow at all times.

My children are now grown and out of the nest. My vocation has turned to supporting those who are called to the ministry of Christian formation, especially on the congregational level in situations similar to the one that I once found myself in. This book is a result of that—the culling together of files, papers, stories, and the nuts and bolts of essentials that I continue to return and refer to. It's not just for the staff person called to the ministry of Christian formation. Youth leaders, volunteers, and yes—even clergy may find this a resource to keep close at hand.

Whether you are new to the ministry of Christian formation or an "old" pro, hopefully the following pages will serve you well and be a handy go-to reference whenever you are in need of a little assistance, whether it be a basic refresher on a church topic, a supply check list, a prayer before a teachers' meeting, or even a laugh when you've experienced a frustrating staff meeting. All of the information contained here is the real stuff. It's been tested and approved just short of receiving the "Good Housekeeping Seal of Approval." If you are new to the Episcopal Church, there is stuff for you to learn about us. If you are new to teaching, you'll find info that teachers need to know.

Your ministry is so important to the life and vibrancy of the Episcopal Church. You are building a faithful future for others and the next generation. You don't need to be bogged down in the nitty-gritty of reinventing the wheel. Hopefully, you'll find that stuff here. Your task is to build those relationships . . . sharing your love of Jesus, God, and the Story.

> *So Sarah laughed to herself, saying, "After I have grown old, and my husband is old, shall I have pleasure?" The* Lord *said to Abraham, "Why did Sarah laugh, and say, 'Shall I indeed bear a child, now that I am old?' Is anything too wonderful for the* Lord*? At the set time I will return to you, in due season, and Sarah shall have a son." But Sarah denied, saying, "I did not laugh"; for she was afraid. He said, "Oh yes, you did laugh."* (Genesis 18:12–15)

Being a Christian educator is very much like giving birth. Have fun. Sometimes you may want to cry, but remember always to laugh. God will certainly put enough interesting challenges in your path and enjoy a chuckle with you.

Sharon Ely Pearson
The Feast of Pentecost 2013

CHRISTIAN ED STUFF

WHAT IS CHRISTIAN FORMATION?

Christian formation is the lifelong journey of growing in faith. With Christ as our companion, we are always on a life-changing journey in our relationships with one another and in our encounter with the Living God. It involves liturgy and worship, service and witness, instruction (scripture and tradition) in connection with education (application to daily life). Formation occurs when the whole community is engaged together, as well as individually, as we discern who God is calling us to be—no matter what our age is. It is holistic and experiential in nature.

As Episcopalians, it is realized in how we live out our Baptismal Covenant. Through prayer, worship, study, fellowship, and mission we can experience spiritual growth in our lives, becoming reconciled to God in Christ as well as our neighbor. As Christian formation leaders, we can encourage others to participate in a life of prayer and study as well as community gatherings that support us in our lifelong journey of faith.

Be prepared. Despite the term "Christian formation" being around for years, you'll still find yourself having to explain it over and over again. Quickly learn your elevator speech to respond at a moment's notice.

SPIRITUAL FORMATION VS. EDUCATION

In the twenty-first century there is a new paradigm for ministry with children and youth. Moving away from the "banking model" in which the church's education mission was to fill the minds of students with correct answers about God, we understand that a spiritual formation model embraces the whole congregation— children, youth, and adults—as partners in learning a life of faith that is ongoing.

The church's educational mission is to provide an environment that cultivates an intimacy with God through one's mind as well as one's heart that continues through the lifespan. Children and youth are recognized as already having a relationship with God, experiencing the holy in their daily lives. Teachers are spiritual guides, pointing to the presence of God through mentoring, discernment, and role modeling. Spiritual practices are experienced via prayer, service, discussion, storytelling, journaling, retreats, and other ways.

Faith is an ongoing process and relationship with God, through Jesus Christ.

WHAT IS A CHRISTIAN EDUCATOR?

Educators serves as directors of Christian education, directors of children's, youth, and/or adult ministries, seminary faculty, day school directors and teachers, resource center directors, church camp directors, as well as a variety of other educational ministries. The ministry of education encompasses roles that help to shape an educational vision, establish goals, evaluate, plan and arrange programs, call leaders, and define and select curricula.

A great Christian educator:

- engages people of all ages and helps them see themselves as Christ's beloved;
- is one who reflects Christ's beliefs and actions;
- is more concerned with what the eyes, ears, nose, mouth, hands, and heart know than what is understood; they are patient because they know, share, and live waiting on God;
- has a clear sense of their own spirituality and joy in awakening the spirituality of others;
- is a great storyteller who can help people of all ages be with God rather than know about God;
- has a sense of humor and the patience to meet, greet, and engage with all sorts of interesting people under circumstances you'd never dream of outside of church—the supermarket, post office, Department of Motor Vehicles, and even jury duty.

THE CALL TO BE A CHRISTIAN EDUCATOR

Teachers are called, first by God, through Jesus Christ. (Matthew 28:19, 20a)

Through Jesus Christ, God has promised to be our constant companion in the task of teaching. (Matthew 28:20b)

When we were baptized into the household of God, we were given the gift of the Holy Spirit. (Acts 2:38–39)

The Holy Spirit blesses those who teach, its "bearers," with the fruit of the Spirit. (Galatians 5:22–23)

Teachers commit themselves to being God's saints: to showing their love for God by serving others—in this case, the children, youth, and adults who take part in Christian education. (Mark 9:36–37)

Teachers help members and friends of the church to fulfill the vows made at baptism—to teach and nurture and love those who are growing in the faith. These are the promises God's people have made for generations. (Psalm 78:5–7)

DIRECTOR OF CHRISTIAN EDUCATION

Christian education is not the responsibility of any one person or committee. Rather, it is a task for every member of the congregation. In his or her own way each person should supply the needed resources and attend to necessary functions. The professional person hired for Christian educational ministries should not be expected to assume the responsibilities of others in the church: clergy, parents, teachers, congregational leaders, participants, etc. Instead, he or she brings trained skill to the church's educational ministry. The director of Christian education (DCE) works with the clergy and with the people of the church, and they, in turn, work with the DCE to accomplish the congregation's overall educational task.

Specific duties usually fall into several categories, including:

Teaching

- Work with young people alongside other teachers, advisors, and leaders.
- Call volunteers for teaching.
- Design and implement teacher training.
- Assume special seasonal planning: Christmas pageant, Lenten and Advent programs, Vacation Bible School (VBS), confirmation, baptism preparation, etc.
- Provide resources for teachers: supplies, materials, curricula, articles, etc.
- Integrate education programs with other formation areas: worship, outreach, mission, pastoral care, stewardship, etc.

Administration

- Maintain a data base of children, youth, and families.
- Communicate with participants, parents, and the congregation following the church's policies and procedures.
- Be an advisor to the Christian Education Committee for selecting curricula and other policy and programming decisions.

- Consult with leaders who have responsibility for formation programs and activities.
- Consult with the clergy and staff regarding Christian education policies and training.

Personal Growth and Development

- Continue education and training in such areas as Safe Church, anti-racism, educational theory, and theology via diocesan offerings or other workshops.
- Read journals, magazines, and new publications.

DIRECTOR OF YOUTH MINISTRIES

As with a DCE, the youth minister is not a pied piper called to have teenagers follow them so others need not be involved. You don't need to be a tech geek or pop music fan, but you need to know how and what youth are connected to and with. Responsibilities often fall into similar categories as those of the DCE, with specific focus on young people ages twelve to eighteen.

Teaching

- Work with young people in the congregation alongside other advisors and leaders.
- Assume any special seasonal responsibilities that may be assigned: worship services, preaching, mission trips, Confirmation, retreats, service and outreach projects.
- Integrate education programs with other areas: worship, outreach, mission, pastoral care, stewardship, etc.

Administration

- Maintain contact with parents.
- Consult with leaders who have responsibility for children's and adult education programs.
- Consult with the clergy and staff regarding Christian education policies and training.
- Provide communication to youth, parents, and the church in general on a regular basis.

Extra Duties

- Participate in, support, and contribute to diocesan, provincial, and church-wide programs as appropriate.
- Attend events that youth may be involved with in the community: school concerts and plays, sports events, etc.

Personal Growth and Development

- Continue education and training in such areas as Safe Church, anti-racism, educational theory, and theology via diocesan offerings or other workshops.
- Read journals, magazines, and new publications.
- Network with colleagues.

YOU'VE GOT THE JOB!

Once you have a position description—use it! Build relationships with other staff and develop allies to support you. Don't forget to be an advocate for yourself!

- Obtain a letter of agreement that specifies hours, salary, benefits, continuing education, and an annual review. Request a title that explains your position.
- Document your hours and what you do in that time.
- Get business cards.
- Dress as a professional.
- Be intentional about establishing relationships with other staff members. Build collegiality and trust.
- Begin meeting persons in the congregation. Call key members to meet for lunch or coffee.
- Attend meetings, even those you are not required to attend, in order to introduce yourself and get to know other leaders in the congregation.
- Make yourself available. Hiding in your office will not help build relationships.
- Form a Christian education committee of eight to ten people (with at least one strong supporter and a vestry representative) if one does not already exist.
- Keep church leadership informed of your work.
- Inventory the territory. You are as responsible for space as you are for people. Go through old files. Make a list of your equipment. Snoop around the classrooms to see what has been used (or unused).

NEW GIRL (OR GUY) IN TOWN

For youth ministers in particular, it is helpful to establish relationships within the local community outside of the church building.

- Become acquainted with the leaders and resources of your deanery, convocation, or diocese.
- Call churches in your area to learn whether they have an educator or youth minister and get to know them.
- Call the principals of the schools your youth attend. Ask if you can make an appointment to meet them and observe classes.
- Go to school events, sports games, dramatic productions, and open houses to be aware of the places and people that are important to your congregation.
- Establish relationships with local social service agencies. They will come in handy when it comes time to plan a service project.
- If there is a college or university near you, get in touch with their campus ministry chaplain.
- Participate in workshops and education events offered by your diocese.
- Learn how you can get your youth involved with other youth groups or diocesan events.

THE 911

This should be the first thing you figure out. There will be a time you set off the church alarm—either in the sacristy, the office, or the whole building. It will happen when you are the only person around.

To prepare for such an event:

- Get the code tattooed on an accessible (but hidden) body part.
- Make sure the phone number that the security company has as a backup is not your home phone; you don't want those late-night calls.
- Call the security company before they call the fire or police department.
- Find out the "secret, secret password" that the security company will ask you. See above.

Instead of the typical alarm system, you may want to suggest to your property committee what is becoming a practice in the Church of England—installing movement sensors that are hidden in spires and finials. The alarms flash blue lights and trigger a booming voice that takes intruders by surprise, warning them that security guards are on their way. There's nothing like the voice of God to scare folks off.

HOW TO CREATE
A DREAM TEAM

Gone are the days (hopefully) when ministries with children, youth, and adults are segregated into their own little fiefdoms. Working in partnership, youth leaders, Sunday school teachers, and adult mentors can collaborate and support one another in providing one seamless voice of advocacy for all ages of formation.

When planning out the program calendar, consult with one another. Work on your budgets together so that youth, children, adults, mission trips, Vacation Bible School, and the Christmas pageant aren't pitted against each other when it comes to budget requests sent to the finance committee and vestry.

After all, children will "feed" into the youth program, and a solid ministry to youth will grow future (and present) leaders of the congregation.

If you're able, outside of whatever staff meeting all of you might attend, gather regularly over coffee (or some other libation) to share ideas, compare notes, grumble to one another about the latest fiasco someone is complaining about, or simply get to know one another more.

Don't divide and conquer—unite and build up the Body of Christ!

MANY PARTS,
BUT ONE BODY

Try not to fall prey to the One-Eared Mickey Mouse model of ministry. It looks like it sounds—a big circle (the church) with another smaller circle (your youth group or church school) that touch but do not overlap. It is a simple drawing that asks: Are youth (or children) treated like a real part of the church?

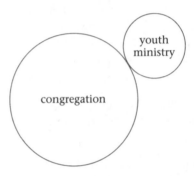

Characteristics of churches where this model does not exist include youth in every aspect of community. Youth are encouraged and invited to serve on committees and boards. Not only are youth invited, they are also listened to and their input is welcomed and sought. Teenagers are smart and know when they are actually wanted and listened to.

In these churches, all ages are included in planning worship. Worship is about the whole of Christ's body connecting together and offering praise and thanks. In many churches it is the only time all age groups are together. Churches that break away from the One-Eared Mickey Mouse make sure that worship is designed with all members in mind.

The heart of the issue of moving children and youth from outside to inside is to make them feel cared for and important. That's important for any group in church.

BUT WE *ALWAYS* HAD SUNDAY SCHOOL!

No we didn't. Sunday school did not begin with Adam and Eve reading Bible stories to Cain and Abel. Jesus didn't hold a Torah School for little children either. Where did this practice come from?

Sunday school didn't begin until the 1800s. Robert Raikes, a devout Anglican layman and newspaper publisher in Glouster, England established a school in "Soot Alley" for poor children of the city as part of his efforts at prison reform in 1803. The purpose was to teach working children the rudiments of learning (reading and math) on Sunday, their free day. And of course, the Bible was a primary tool for teaching. No separation of church and state back then!

Sunday school associations were formed to carry on the work and the movement found its fullest expression in the United States, beginning in Philadelphia in 1824 with the Sunday School Society. It spread to the frontier (west of the Appalachian Mountains) with readers, song books, Bibles, and other materials in saddlebags, making Sunday school an established part of each pioneer village at an early stage of its development.

Its roots were with the concern of social uplift (personal hygiene, literacy, and personal morality), evangelization of the unsaved, or the education of believers in the faith. Lots of changes have occurred since then, but this is enough of a history lesson. Toothbrush in one hand, Bible in the other!

NEEDS VS. WANTS

Evaluating and selecting curricular resources may be one of the most important tasks of a Christian educator (besides being a role model and spiritual guide). Each congregation is different with its own needs and desires—one size does not fit all! Remember that what they want is not necessarily what they need.

It is important for more than one person to evaluate and choose a curriculum, whether it is for children, youth, or adults. A committee should be formed that includes clergy, Christian education director or administrator, parents, and teachers who provide educational leadership. If materials for youth are being considered, there should be at least two youth also involved.

Mission

- ◆ What is your congregation's mission statement or vision?
- ◆ How can curriculum support it?

Bible

- ◆ What are the biblical needs of your congregation?
- ◆ Are members familiar with the Bible and key stories or is basic instruction needed?
- ◆ Is there a desire to integrate faith with daily living?

Priorities

- ◆ What is most important . . .
    - ◇ Gospel-based, outreach- and mission–focused, and/or worship-centered?
    - ◇ Doctrinal teachings and creedal statements that reflect the Episcopal Church?
    - ◇ Communication for linking home and church?
    - ◇ Ease of use: lesson plans, preparation time, and age appropriate content?
    - ◇ Aesthetics: quality of materials, artwork, website, music, layout of lesson?

◇ Sociological: roles of people, racial inclusiveness and diversity, historical perspectives and accuracy?

Teachers

◆ Are your teachers experienced or new?
◆ What support do they need for teaching the curriculum?

Attendance

◆ What are the attendance patterns?
◆ What are the implications of quarterly, weekly, or seasonal units of study?

EXPLICIT AND IMPLICIT

We often understand curriculum in a narrow sense, seeing it only as a set of materials—the books for teachers and students. It is more accurate to speak of these as curricular materials and resources, recognizing that they are only part of the whole curriculum for education in the church.

Since we are learning all the time, we also must be aware of all that is going into our design for learning. Part of choosing the right curricular materials involves understanding:

> *The Explicit Curriculum*—What we present, consciously and with intention, including the materials we purchase for teaching lessons is easily recognizable.

> *The Implicit Curriculum*—How we present our lessons is often hidden. How is the room designed? What learning styles do we tap into? What is our attitude about teaching as well as our love of the Bible? This is the unspoken curriculum.

Jesus' teaching was not based on memorization, repetition and recitation, but rather on spontaneous creative responses to situations and experiences. Curricular work is holy work, religious work, and God dwells with us as we do it, in the midst of it all.

WHAT IS *THE* CURRICULUM?

In the Acts of the Apostles (2:42, 44–47), Luke describes the course of the church's life—its purpose and its actions. We can think of this as the church's curriculum. The word "curriculum" comes from the Latin verb *currere*, which means "to run." Taken literally, curriculum means a course to be run, just as the early church lived out its existence. Today it is much the same; the curriculum is our total experience of Christian education and formation. It involves every facet of discipleship, at every age, when we:

Proclaim the word of Jesus' resurrection (*Kerygma*)

Teach the sacred story and its meaning to our lives (*Didache*)

Come together to pray and re-present Jesus in the breaking of the bread (*Leiturgia*)

Living in community with one another (*Koinonia*)

Care for those in need (*Diakonia*)

Broadly defined, curriculum is the design or plan for Christian education in the congregation.

TYPES OF CURRICULUM

Curricular materials come in a variety of formats for teaching in the Christian education setting. Each addresses content using a scope (range) and sequence (order) as well as process for teaching. For use, they range from needing teacher training to lesson plans that are included for immediate implementation. The following are the most common types produced from publishers:

Lectionary Based—Follows the Sunday readings (lections) each week that are used in worship, usually following the Gospel and the Revised Common Lectionary (RCL) on a three-year cycle.

Bible Story Based—Old Testament and New Testament stories are told in sequential order that loosely follow the seasons of the church year. Each age level may follow a different story in a two- or three-year cycle.

Learning Centers—Often known as "workshop" or "rotation," this model taps into the various learning styles in how the biblical story is presented; students explore one story for several weeks through a variety of means such as art, music, drama, computers, cooking, science, etc.

Montessori/Worship Centered—Experiential in nature, this type of curriculum uses silence, wondering, and personal response, allowing the student to learn liturgical language with the guidance of a storyteller/teacher who shares the biblical story using hands-on materials.

Thematic—Follows a topic, issue, or interest for several weeks (or sometimes months) for in-depth study. This type of curricula is often used with youth and adults.

HOW TO PLAN THE YEAR

Sometimes it feels as though the calendar drives our lives. As much as we would like to throw it out the window, the calendar is important in planning. Pay close attention to several calendars: the Christian calendar, your church's calendar of annual events, and the local school calendar.

With a blank calendar, begin blocking out dates that you know are immovable feasts—Christmas, Easter, the annual meeting, church picnic, winter vacation, secular holidays, plus any other idiosyncrasies of your community.

Meet with your church's staff (or volunteers) to plan your Christian education calendar. If possible, having everyone sitting around the same table to map out the year can avoid conflicts and stress as the year progresses. You'll want to make sure you've got dibs on dates for the following:

+ Rally Day (aka beginning of program year)
+ Teacher commissioning
+ Teacher meetings and trainings
+ Pageants and rehearsals
+ Special seasonal events
+ Vacation Bible School
+ You know what to add to this list!

THE CHURCH SCHOOL TEACHER

The role of a Church School or Sunday school teacher is to assist in the nurture, care and spiritual feeding of children in a Church School setting, being a wholesome example of the Body of Christ. Through the telling of God's story (using curriculum) a teacher is offered the opportunity to share his or her own faith.

Qualifications

- a personal relationship with Jesus Christ
- a desire to grow in faith by regular Bible reading and prayer
- a commitment to regularly attend worship
- completion of a background check
- completion of Safe Church training

Responsibilities

- Guide learning by:
  - being well prepared with a lesson;
  - selecting a variety of learning activities;
  - participating in appropriate ways with children in activities.
- Arrive fifteen minutes before students.
- Greet each child upon arrival.
- Model the love of Christ by getting to know each child.

RETHINKING RECRUITMENT

Cross off the word "recruitment" from your vocabulary. Replace it with "calling for ministry."

Unhelpful assumptions:

* Any warm body will do.
* If you are a parent, you have a vested interest in having a church school.
* The only possible contribution is to be a "teacher" in a class.
* You have to know the subject matter and then you have to teach it—all by yourself. But . . .
* You do not necessarily need to know the material very well.
* Being a church school volunteer is reward enough in itself.

Expand your vision:

* Who seems to have rapport with young people?
* Who includes children in their conversations?
* Who are your storytellers or musicians?
* Who are the church's living saints?
* Who do you think of when the words faith, spirit, and character are mentioned?
* Who is eagerly learning about their faith?
* Who acknowledges they don't have all the answers?

HOW TO CALL VOLUNTEERS

We all have gifts, graces, and talents given to us by God. As Christians, we are called to serve God and use these gifts, graces, and talents. You call people to service and to share their gifts through ministries of teaching and learning in your congregation. It is a call to ministry.

Develop a team. If at all possible, have more than one person involved in the task of identifying teachers and leaders. Working as a team, it is often easier to identify gifts and talents. As you prepare to contact persons, remember:

- Approach the task of identifying potential teachers and leaders with prayer.
- Be open to people who may not immediately come to mind.
- Talk with each person you invite.
- List the gifts and talents you see in each person you are asking. List how these can be used in the ministry you are proposing to them.
- Be honest. Give a realistic idea of the time needed, the length of service (including when it will end), and what support they can expect from the church.
- Take time to explain the ministry thoroughly, including any information you think might help the person know more about what you're asking him or her to do.
- Give your personal experience and appraisal of the rewards and downsides.
- Be enthusiastic. Teaching is an important job.
- Give people time for thought and prayer.
- Be persistent. Honor absolute "no's." Listen for indications that the person might be interested.

Communicate. Pray. Let the whole church know you are discerning who might be called to the ministry of teaching. Simply putting an announcement in the bulletin or making a verbal plea usually brings out the "usual suspects" and often those who do not have the right skills or appropriate attributes you are seeking. Lift up the needs in your Sunday prayers during worship.

Keep, O Lord, your household the Church in your steadfast faith and love, that through your grace we may proclaim your truth with boldness, and minister your justice with compassion. Keep our hearts and minds open to discern the gifts that you have given all of your people, so that we may find those who are called to teach and learn with our children, youth, and adults. Send us those who have a love for Your Word and children (or youth) that they can support us in our ministry as teachers and learners; through Jesus Christ our Lord, who lives and reigns with you and the Holy Spirit, one God, forever and ever. Amen.

—ADAPTED FROM THE *1979* BOOK OF COMMON PRAYER, P. *230*

HOW TO NURTURE THOSE IN THE TRENCHES

The church is the largest volunteer organization in the world. How do you support those volunteers?

- Have clear goals and expectations of what they will do.
- Be flexible! Have volunteer projects on weekends and weekdays, mornings and evenings.
- Make sure volunteers understand the importance of the task they are doing and how it fits into the overall mission of the church.
- Never allow people to feel that you wasted their time or that they weren't really needed.
- Provide food and refreshments whenever possible.
- Remember the birthdays of committed volunteers.
- Provide a structure so that those who want to can take on roles of greater responsibility.
- Give honest and sincere praise. Say "thank you."
- Make the specific project an "event"—make it more interesting than staying home and watching it.
- Recognize volunteers publicly: weekly bulletin, newsletter, website, meetings, etc.
- Have parties, retreats, picnics, and other "off-duty" events to celebrate ministries and fellowship.
- Give volunteers titles if appropriate—coordinator, assistant coordinator, lead organizer, etc.

WE NEED S'MORE TEACHERS

Dear Church School Teacher,

With you as our teacher, we have . . .

- ◆ Learned s'more.
- ◆ Laughed s'more.
- ◆ Done s'more.
- ◆ Grown in faith s'more.

Thank you for making us s'more than we would have been without you! We appreciate you s'more than you know! We need s'more teachers like you!

Top a graham cracker with a piece of chocolate and marshmallow. Arrange on a microwavable plate and microwave on high for fifteen to twenty seconds or until marshmallow puffs. Top with a second graham cracker and press slightly together to secure. Enjoy!

> With love,
> From the children of our two churches

This message was delivered to over a hundred volunteer teachers along with a baggie of ingredients by Becky Hudspeth and Sheri Richards, children's ministries co-coordinators for St. Matthew's Episcopal Church and Wilton Presbyterian Church in Wilton, Connecticut.

HOW TO EVALUATE
A RESOURCE

When reviewing curricular resources, ask the following questions. Make sure to review different age levels and several sessions.

- What is the theology of the material? What are the assumptions regarding the teacher and students' relationship to God?
- What is the mode of learning basic to Christian formation for this education program? Does it encompass Scripture, tradition, and reason?
- What is the end goal for the individual (student and teacher)? How is discipleship built through the materials?
- What type of curriculum is this (lectionary, story-based, Montessori, etc.)? What are the needs of your church regarding the type of curriculum chosen?
- How does the material relate to daily life?
- What is the expectation for teacher knowledge about child development and learning?
- What are the expectations for teacher preparation?
- What is the role of the teacher? Guide, facilitator, mentor, administrator, authority?
- Is there any provision included for teacher training?
- How is Scripture presented (literally, open for interpretation, etc.)?
- What is the language for God? Inclusive?
- Do the suggested lesson-related activities provide for student interaction in a variety of expressions, using different learning styles?
- Are the different age levels comparable in format, content, and theology?
- Is there a component for worship?
- How does the material relate to your church, community, and the world?
- What are the basic costs? Are there any hidden costs, such as the need to purchase special art supplies or supplemental materials?

HOW TO ASSESS
YOUR SPACE

Take a look at the big picture of your facilities and your education and formation ministries. Spend some time with an open mind and open heart. Dream. Plan for the future and what might be. It is important to do everything possible to make all available space conducive for learning for all users and ages.

Make a list of all the users of each space.
Look at the space and ask:

+ How many children (youth, adults) are there per class/meeting?
+ What are their ages?
+ What are their developmental needs for space?
+ What accessibility needs do they have (ramps, elevator, signs, bathrooms, exits)?
+ Are there lots of tables and other furniture in the space that could be moved to allow more room for movement?
+ Are there lots of doors? Close some off if this will not be a threat to safety.
+ Are there any big or bulky chairs or fixed seats? Move those out and move in smaller, movable chairs. Or move out all the chairs and use the floor, if appropriate for the group.

Planning the meeting space:

+ Small children need small chairs that do not fold and small tables (coffee tables work!).
+ Children also need rooms without fancy rugs so that glitter and paint can be used with abandon.
+ Adding lights or using brighter bulbs makes a room more cheerful and cuts down on eyestrain. Clean windows help too!
+ Painting rooms white, ivory, or eggshell makes them brighter and friendlier. Bright colors can be overstimulating to young children.

- Rug scraps and big pillows can be arranged to make a cozy story-corner for children. Some carpet distributors will give away discontinued stock samples.
- Collect posters from organizations that focus on the needs of the world and old wall calendars that can be mounted on poster board and "framed" with a contrasting color of poster board.
- Children prefer large, indoor classrooms that allow social participation.
- Classrooms with older children, youth, and adults should avoid seating in rows. A circle of chairs or a grouping around a table encourages two-way communication.
- Floors of rooms used by children should be clean, un-slippery, smooth, and free from safety hazards.
- Hot water pipes and radiators should be covered by permanent screen guards or insulation.
- Room temperatures should be maintained at not less than 68° F when it is below freezing outside and not more than the outside temperature if it is above 80° F.
- The basic classroom should have at least 72 square feet of windows for natural light.

HOW TO ASSESS
YOUR EQUIPMENT

Besides taking care of your personal body, mind, and spirit you may also be in charge of the care and upkeep of educational space and equipment—its suitability, functioning, and cleanliness (just like your body).

Regularly make a plan for assessing the space and equipment, considering these possibilities:

- Find someone to do a thorough check of all electronic equipment, inventorying serial numbers and identifying needed repair work or replacement of parts (LCD projectors, DVD players, TVs, etc.).

- Put together a small team to make a thorough inventory of all classrooms and facilities used by Christian education. Assess cleanliness, need for repair or painting, suitability for groups, need for replacement or repair of furnishings, and the removal of broken, unsafe, or unused equipment and resources.

- Ask a group of parents to give an eagle eye to the church nursery, cleaning and/or clearing out toys as well as checking out furnishings with an eye toward safety for wee ones.

- Form a team to review supply areas, making note of closets, storage cabinets, and containers. Reorganize and label as needed.

- Make a wish list for electronic equipment, toys, art supplies, and furnishings that church members might choose to give.

HOW TO MANAGE A CROWD

Kindergarteners are lined up in the hall to enter a classroom because the room is full. Fourth graders are sitting on windowsills because you've run out of chairs. Youth are on strike to meet in your roomy (ha!) office. It's nice to have this problem, but sometimes even with small enrollment in education programs, the sizes of the classrooms from our eighteenth-century buildings don't seem to work.

Here are some widely accepted standards:

Age Level	Minimum Room Size
K–3rd Grade	750–1,350 sq. ft.
4th–8th Grade	660–1,000 sq. ft.
9th–12th Grade	600 sq. ft.

Age in years	Teacher to Child	Max. per Room
Infants–1 year	1:3 or 4	6 in arms
2- and 3-year-olds	1:5	12
4- and 5-year-olds	1:6	12
6–8-year-olds	1:10	15
9–12-year-olds	1:12	15

Thirty-five square feet per child is a 5' x 7' space—a little over twice the dimensions of the average playpen. Minimum standards for prisons require more than 35 square feet per prisoner.

A SUCCESSFUL TEACHERS' (OR ANY) MEETING

Before the meeting:

- Establish an agenda that allows for dialogue, reflection, and decision-making.
- Check the date, time, and location to avoid conflicts.
- Send out a reminder to participants.

At the meeting:

- Begin on time (with prayer).
- Include a reflection or activity that strengthens participants' relationships with God, one another, and the ministry.
- Designate someone to take notes.
- Adjust the agenda as needed.
- Ask for feedback.

After the meeting:

- Review your notes.
- Send out minutes to remind others of the tasks they committed to do.
- Touch base with individuals for clarity (of the above).
- Thank those who offered a report or assistance.
- Reflect on who else needs to be in the communication loop.
- Begin building the agenda for the next meeting.

AGENDA: FORMATION STYLE

Gathering

Create a ritual that focuses your group on your purpose. Light a candle, sing a song, read a piece of Scripture (perhaps related to an item on your agenda), tell a story, allow for silence, say a prayer.

Touching Base

Offer the opportunity for each person to speak for two or three minutes (that's the challenge) of where they have "been" since the last meeting. Sharing hopes of what this meeting will accomplish sets the tone.

Business

This is where the group addresses the items that need to be discussed such as Vacation Bible School plans, visioning, curriculum selection, new families, service projects, etc.

Closing

At the end of the meeting focus attention on how God has been present in your gathering. Express prayers of gratitude and intercession as everyone is sent forth to live out their ministry in God's creation.

THE TWO-ADULT RULE

Our churches are trusting environments that have not traditionally been a place where adults were carefully screened and monitored. But the world has changed, and when we are involved in children and youth ministry, our programs are representing the church. For children and youth, this often represents their image of God.

Mantra: Two-adult rule at all times!

Everyone who works with children and youth (teachers, drivers, chaperones, mentors) should take the Safe Church training recommended by your diocese. For some, this is *Safeguarding God's Children*. For others, it is a program designed and offered by the diocese. Volunteers must understand that part of their responsibility is to help keep children safe. Training and background checks make a difference. Those who attend training are always glad they did.

Steps we must take to keep our ministries safe include:

+ Screening
+ Interacting
+ Monitoring
+ Training
+ Responding

WHY BACKGROUND CHECKS?

Having a policy of background checks for all adults who work with children and youth in our churches is important in today's world. In addition to our promise to live out our Baptismal Covenant (BCP, p. 304), here's why:

> *And you will have confidence, because there is hope; you will be protected and take your rest in safety.* (Job 11:18)

Loving young people and wanting to work with them is the reason we are all involved in ministries with children and youth. In order to create the safest possible environment for our love and affection, it is important that we act as role models and leaders in our churches and communities.

> *And those who know your name put their trust in you, for you, O LORD, have not forsaken those who seek you.* (Psalm 9:10)

Our churches are trusting environments that have not traditionally been a place where adults were carefully screened and monitored. But the world has changed, and when we are involved in children and youth ministry, our programs are representing the church. For children and youth, this often represents their image of God.

> *You then, my child, be strong in the grace that is in Christ Jesus; and what you have heard from me through many witnesses entrust to faithful people who will be able to teach others as well.* (2 Timothy 2:1–2)

Volunteers must understand that part of their responsibility is to help keep children safe. Training and background checks make a difference.

THE CHURCH NURSERY

This ministry of your church should be tops on the list as it provides care for some of the most vulnerable members of our congregations. It can also be a "thumbs up" or "thumbs down" first impression for new families.

Guidelines for a Safe Nursery

- Establish a committee to oversee this ministry with a regular schedule for checking, cleaning, and replacing toys and other nursery equipment.

- Screen everyone who has access to the children and youth in your church. Follow the practice of two adults present at all times, having windows in entrance doors, and having diaper changing stations in central locations.

- Always have an adult in charge. It is best if the same person is there each week. Require all nursery workers to go through an orientation before working in the nursery.

- Minimum adult–to-child ratio recommendations:

  - 1 adult to 3 infants
  - 1 adult to 4 toddlers
  - 1 adult to 6 children 3 years and older

- Make sure toys are age appropriate. If a toy (or its parts) fits through a toilet paper tube, do not use.

- Regularly check floors for choking hazards such as: coins, marbles, safety pins, jewelry, buttons, crayons, pen caps, nails, screws, etc.

- Avoid stuffed animals, as they are great germ carriers.

- Practice SIDS prevention: always put infants to bed on their backs.

- Check that mattresses used are firm and flat; do not use blankets or pillows in the crib. Crib sheets should cover the mattress snugly. If a sheet comes off easily when you pull at the corners or sides, do not use it. Have clean crib sheets readily available and have a plan for making sure used crib linens and changing table covers are washed and returned each week.

- Make sure that crib slats are spaced properly. You should not be able to pass a can of soda between the slats of a crib. They should not have cutouts in the end panels or corner posts and should be placed away from windows.
- Make sure all electrical cords are out of the way and all electrical outlets are covered.
- Tie up window-blind cords.
- Post emergency exits and phone numbers including poison control. Have fire drills on a regular basis.
- Always make sure children are seated while eating.
- Have non-toxic cleaning supplies readily available to nursery workers but well out of the reach of children.
- Check premises for adequate ventilation and test for the presence of lead, especially in buildings built before 1970.
- If there is no sink in the room, have disinfectant hand cleaners available for caregivers.
- Don't get too comfortable: keep checking and revising your nursery policies.

FEE OR FREE?

To charge or not to charge—that seems to be the big question these days as budgets get tight and pledging goes down.

Churches differ about charging registration fees for programs. Some charge the participants in a program exactly what it costs to run the program, while others charge no registration fee at all and build all expenses into the church budget. Another alternative is to view each program or event independently, according to the type of program it is.

Christian education is usually part of the annual church budget with a focus on Church School including youth and adult classes. If a resource is needed in adult study, individuals may purchase their own books.

Youth ministry is often a different line item, but individuals usually pay for the registration for the annual ski trip. Finances should never keep anyone from participating in an activity or program, so scholarships should always be made available for any event a church sponsors.

If a registration fee for a program can break the bank (such as a mission trip or pilgrimage), fund-raisers help offset costs. A good recipe to follow for dividing costs for youth is ⅓ church, ⅓ family, ⅓ individual (that is, the youth).

DON'T HIDE IT UNDER A BUSHEL

You know the song "This Little Light of Mine." Don't let Satan *phift* it out—let others know what great things you are doing in your educational ministries. You don't need to be a marketing expert, but you do need to be a good communicator.

Bulletin Boards

Yes, they are "old school," but placed in strategic locations (near entrances, outside your office, near the coffee) they can attract attention and share the latest fliers of events, schedules, photographs, and artwork. But refresh it at least once a quarter! There's nothing like faded construction paper to say, "Nothing new is going on here." To really be on the cutting edge, use a monitor screen with a running loop of announcements for people to view as they walk by heavy traffic areas.

Fliers

Need to share a brief announcement? Pageant rehearsal schedule? Permission slips for the mission trip due? Don't inundate folks with paper that they won't take home—place colorful fliers in spots people will notice—the backs of doors on bathroom stalls, on the refrigerator, on an easel in the narthex.

E-News

There are several inexpensive and easy-to-use ways to send an e-mail blast to your parents, families, or the entire congregation. The key is making sure they are visually appealing with great graphics and brief on words. Send recipients to your website with a quick link for more information.

WHEN'S A YOUTH
NOT A YOUTH?

Children, teenagers, youth, young people, tweens—what language are we using?

For some it doesn't make a difference, but sometimes (especially when it comes to budget and programming) it does. It is also an important distinction for parents and anyone looking for a new church home. Encourage the use of specific age descriptions in your church, especially with leadership. Clumping everyone under the age of twenty-five as a young person doesn't recognize their uniqueness or their particular abilities and needs.

Some helpful groupings:

- ◆ Children are those under the age of twelve.
- ◆ Tweens are a "new" category of those who don't want to be known as children, but aren't teenagers yet (roughly ages nine through twelve).
- ◆ Youth are those between thirteen and eighteen years (aka teenagers).
- ◆ Young adults can be single or married, in college or not, with or without children, living with parents or out on their own. In today's world, they can be between eighteen and thirty years old.
- ◆ Adults sometimes act like any of the above "categories." They do not always make the best role models or mentors, either. Adults need to act like adults.
- ◆ The Canons of the Episcopal Church define an adult member of the church to be a member 16 years or older (see Canon 17.1.b). So that means "voice and vote."

WHAT DO YOU MEAN, "CRADLE TO GRAVE"?

The church is one of the remaining institutions in our society that is a gathering place of many generations under one roof. Generally, parents lack opportunities to be with their children in an educational setting; children and youth have few occasions to interact with senior adults, especially if grandparents live halfway across the country.

Providing multi-generational events and opportunities to mix things up are great ways to pass along the faith from one generation to another.

- Worship together.
- Offer seasonal celebrations that include meals.
- Schedule fellowship times before and after worship.
- Organize family retreats.
- Start adoptive grandparent programs that pair children or youth with a senior adult in your congregation or a senior community.
- Offer intergenerational events where family units or individuals can move from activity station to station following instructions provided at each center.
- Sponsor dramatic presentations such as the Christmas pageant that include all ages.
- Invite elders to read stories to children in classrooms or the nursery.
- Organize service projects that involve all ages working together.

HOW IS STEWARDSHIP FORMATIONAL?

One's understanding of personal stewardship is a continuing journey that should begin in childhood. Most children already have a sense of how to respond with thanksgiving to God who created them and the world in which they live. Theirs is an "attitude of abundance," according to John Westerhoff, when discussing healthy stewardship with children in *Will Our Children Have Faith?* (San Francisco: Harper & Row, 1983). The question is not only "How can we teach stewardship to children?" but "How can we encourage children to continually respond to God's creation by caring and enjoying what God has given them, personally and in the world around them?"

In teaching stewardship with all God's children, it is helpful to build upon the concept through different focal points:

- stewardship of creation
- stewardship of ourselves and our bodies
- stewardship of talents and spiritual gift
- stewardship of time and priorities
- stewardship of our relationship with others
- stewardship of treasure and material possessions

HOW TO INCLUDE SERVICE AND MISSION

All ages grow together in faith when serving together in mission. Plan at least one church-wide mission project a year while also providing ongoing opportunities for service throughout the year.

- Recycle cans and bottles with proceeds designated to a local project.
- Collect used clothing and food pantry items.
- Make food baskets and deliver them to those in need.
- Paint or fix up homes of elderly or infirm members.
- Visit those who are homebound on a regular basis.
- Grow a community garden for a soup kitchen.
- Record "books on tape" for the blind or elderly.
- Participate in the Souper Bowl of Caring on Super Bowl Sunday (*www.souperbowl.org*).
- Participate in "30-Hour Famine" (*www.30hourfamine.org*).
- Participate in a "Walk for Hunger" such as *http://hunger.cwsglobal.org* or another "walk for a cause."
- Hold a rake-a-thon during the autumn.

TOURIST, MISSIONARY, OR PILGRIM?

Youth love to take trips. Getting away from home to be able to hang out with peers on a road trip can bring out the best and worst of anyone.

Tourism is about enjoying a new location, taking in the sites, and purchasing the T-shirt or shot glass to commemorate the trip. Think: Great Adventure and Disney World.

Mission trips for youth (or any age) can provide for life-changing adventures and spiritual awakenings. Organized trips with the intention of serving another person either locally or across the country is putting one's faith into action in a concrete way. Think: Rebuilding houses.

Pilgrimages are all about the spiritual journey. The focus is on getting out of one's usual surroundings in search of Christ. Think: The desert, a cathedral, off the beaten path.

Where to begin?

+ Set goals grounded in a purpose—fun, service, prayer.
+ Create a plan—date, budget, location, transportation.
+ Gather leadership—chaperones, on-site contacts.
+ Look out—for God at all times and in all places.

Reflection at the end of each day:

+ Where did you see Jesus today?
+ How is God still speaking though what you did today?
+ How did Jesus use your hands today?

SOCCER, BAND, HOCKEY, AND THE DEBATE TEAM

Yes, in today's world Sunday mornings now compete with the extra-curricular activities that all of our families are connected to in some form or fashion. The reality is that the world is not the same place as it once was; organized activities for our children and youth have replaced the "go out and play and come home at dinner time" mantra of the local neighborhood and playground.

How can we provide faithful support as educators under such circumstances? Keith Anderson, co-author of *Click 2 Save* (Morehouse, 2012), writes on his blog *http://pastorkeithanderson.net:*

> Rather than wishing away the changes in culture, but far from simply accommodating them, let's find a third way to talk about the life of faith, one in which parents can see all the shuttling around they do, the homework help, getting kids dressed, and, yes, even watching their kid play hockey on Sunday morning as ministry in and of itself. Let's make their time at church something that renews and strengthens them for ministry of family and parent, rather than making them feel guilty for wanting to be at their kids' games.

How can we take our ministry beyond the church building knowing that God is present in neighborhoods, playgrounds, and soccer fields? Do we need alternative models outside of Sunday morning? What would that look like in your congregation?

HOW TO BE BEST FRIENDS
WITH THE ALTAR GUILD

If you want to know who is really in charge of worship, just speak to a member of the Altar Guild. In bygone years this elite group was comprised of the matriarchs of your church. These folks know where everything is and basically make sure the clergy set the altar properly. And if you show up in their home turf (the sacristy) with a pair of white gloves on, showing an interest in their ministry, you can reap great benefits.

You can tap into them for a variety of things:

* locating matches
* learning how to remove stains from any fabric
* giving "tours" to kids to show them where all the implements of worship are kept
* coming to your classroom as a guest speaker to demonstrate the difference between brass and silver and how to polish each
* engaging your class in baking the Eucharistic bread
* making sure your Children's Chapel has an Advent wreath with new candles every year
* teaching confirmands how to "vest" a chalice and wear Eucharistic vestments (in case they're interested)

And don't forget to introduce them to the acolytes. Instruct the acolytes to be nice to them and always smile, or else face their wrath when showing up in sneakers.

HOW TO WELCOME CHILDREN IN WORSHIP

Including children in the worshipping community is grounded in our Baptism—we are all full members of the Body of Christ in the church. Besides their presence, children have much to offer in their participation and contributions to our liturgy. Whether participating in the congregation, in ministerial roles, or as contributors to the writing of liturgy, children's voices and presence complete the whole family of God in worship.

Children can minister in many ways, including:

- singing in a choir
- serving as an usher or greeter with their parent
- serving as an acolyte
- serving as a lector; reading a lesson or prayers
- participating in chancel dramas or pageants

Providing age appropriate materials for children during worship also makes them feel welcome. Create an area in your narthex for children (and parents) with items such as:

- worship bulletins made especially for young readers
- a bookrack filled with quality pictures books that have spiritual themes
- cloth bags (filled with a baggie of crayons, scrap paper for drawing, a soft toy, laminated flash cards of church objects, pipe cleaners, etc.) placed in a large basket
- a rocking chair for an adult to comfort a fussy infant or one who needs a quick feeding

HOW TO GIVE
A CHILDREN'S SERMON

Hopefully, your sermons are so engaging that the whole congregation is held in rapt attention, no matter their age. If you absolutely need to gather children at your feet for their own message, here are some tips.

Do:

- Understand the developmental characteristics of the children you are speaking with.
- Have a clearly articulated theology of children.
- Tell the Story!!!!
- Focus on feelings by asking wondering questions.
- Sit with the children, but don't tower over them.
- Use a conversational tone, but don't "talk down" to them.
- End with a prayer.

Don't:

- Use objects or props. Children are concrete thinkers and won't understand your clever metaphor.
- Begin with a question. That's confusing, insults a child's intelligence, and puts them on the spot. It usually elicits silence or an answer that gets laughter (which is also disrespectful).
- Interpret the story. Again, children don't need anyone to tell them what it means.
- Try to entertain.
- Be sarcastic. Remember, you're with children!

WHEN THE ACOLYTE'S HAIR CATCHES FIRE

The word "acolyte" comes from the Greek word *akolouthos*, meaning companion or helper. The acolyte ministry dates back to the Old Testament, when the prophet Samuel is seen assisting Eli, the Levite priest.

Being an acolyte means you get to handle fire, which is a big draw to young people. Acolytes assist in worship by lighting and extinguishing altar candles, among other duties. Since ancient times, light and fire have reminded people that God is here with us. When acolytes bring the light (fire) into the sanctuary, they are reminding people that God is with us in our worship. After all, Moses saw God in the burning bush.

Unexpected things happen in worship services all the time. Babies cry, people pick their noses during prayers, mobile phones go off, someone dozes off during the sermon and starts to snore, and occasionally an acolyte sets their eyebrows on fire. Teach them how to pat it out, look around to see if anyone noticed, and then continue to worship as if nothing happened.

We church people try to put together rituals and practices that are high and mighty and point to cosmic truths. We are also silly creatures who are prone to doing the exact opposite of what we intended. We are a people of water. We need to be careful of what we do with fire.

HOW TO LEAD
CHILDREN'S CHAPEL

For some congregations, a time and place is set apart for children to participate in their own liturgy that is geared especially for them, often taking place during the Liturgy of the Word in their own space instead of the "big" church.

Children's liturgy is not children's play. Children want to be co-creators in worship; with enthusiastic adult leadership, they can. Storytelling, hands-on participation, and music create a worship experience that helps any age engage in liturgy—the work of the people.

- *Gather together:* Begin with an entrance rite or song. And it doesn't have to be happy-clappy.
- *Proclaim God's Word:* Share one of the lessons of the day though storytelling, drama, pictures, or a children's Bible. There are lots of lectionary-based resources and websites to help you here.
- *Respond to God's Word:* Offer a brief reflection on the biblical story—objects always help! Try to make this interactive. Children will fall into the pattern of answering "Jesus" or "God" to every question if you're not keeping them on their toes.
- *Pray:* Offer children an opportunity to share "glads" and "sads"—things they are thankful for and things that weigh on their hearts. Be prepared for lots of prayers about animals and grandparents.
- *Share the Peace:* Provide a time for them to greet one another before being sent forth.—Thanks be to God!

HOW TO BUILD FAITH AT HOME

We live in a time when families are struggling to survive. Parents work full-time and turn to the church to teach their children about God. Families are busy and children are involved in many activities that take them away from attending church school and worship every week. We have the responsibility to support families by providing them with the resources to make their homes fertile ground for faithful living.

- **Offer classes for parents** when their children are in church school focusing on parenting skills and how to pass along their faith, including how to pray as a family.
- **Provide Advent and Lenten activity calendars** for the home.
- **Have children prepare special prayers** for grace at meals and for bedtime along with a calendar of Bible stories to be read on a weekly basis.
- **Provide a lending library** of quality children's literature with biblical themes or Christian values for children to borrow and read together at home.
- **Send home simple worksheets** to continue the church school lesson at home. You can also e-mail them to all families, catching those who may have been absent.
- **Provide intergenerational events**, especially during Advent and Lent, when objects can be made to take and use as a spiritual practice at home.

HOW TO COVET
DEDICATED SPACE

Sharing rooms with "outside" organizations (a nursery school, a twelve-step program, scouts) that use your building during the week or many groups using the same space on a Sunday can create some challenges to your learning environments. Be creative!

* Add noise-deadening materials to absorb sound in the area (carpet, fabric, acoustic tiles).
* Hang a bed sheet on the wall and pin or tape artwork to "hide" another program's materials or shelves during your class time.
* Use dividers to break visibility and create personal group space (these can also be used as bulletin boards and block areas you wish to hide from view).
* Remove unnecessary furniture that takes up space.
* Put classroom supplies on a rolling cart or portable shelving on wheels that can be whisked to a secure location during the week.

THE "CLASSROOM" OF THE FUTURE

Traditional academic classrooms may largely disappear in the future, replaced by holistic learning labs and exploratory centers. To support this trend and approach, classrooms must be multi-purpose, allowing a blending of traditional instruction with meaningful and diverse hands-on, lab-type experiences that include everything from multi-media use to dramatic arts.

A physical environment that stimulates creativity and fosters a sense of belonging will stand the test of time. Classrooms used during the day (Sunday) may also be occupied by community organizations at night.

Educators and congregational planners need to keep in mind that children's needs and populations change, and when they do, spatial requirements change with them. The "one-size-fits-all" classroom model is disappearing, and a quest for more flexible and adaptable classroom configurations should be part of any building planning process.

And yes, smart boards, wireless connectivity, and tweeting in the classroom have already arrived.

HOW TO USE TECHNOLOGY

We may be digital immigrants, but the children and youth in our programs are digital natives—they have always been connected! While the face-to-face and personal relationships are foundational to our formation ministries, the use of technology is important to use in teaching.

The key to using any technology (a computer, website, movie, music, camera or iPad, etc.) is to test it out *before* your class. Make sure you view movies and listen to music ahead of time, not just at the suggestion of your class as it may turn your face red when you realize it's a bit more risqué than WWJD.

- **Use the Internet.** If your church is wireless, you have the world at your fingertips in the classroom. Visit websites of biblical locations or biographies of saints.

- **View movie clips.** Watch a YouTube video or a clip from a movie to illustrate a concept. A great source for film, music, or art is *www.textweek.com.*

- ***Digital cameras*** allow you to capture contemporary images, create montages, or film stories written by students.

- **Take advantage of web-based curriculum.** More and more published material is now totally online, allowing for additional interactive games and activities plus links to other web content to enhance your lessons.

"WHATCHA GONNA DO WHEN THEY COME FOR YOU?"

"Bad boy, bad boy, whatcha gonna do? Whatcha gonna do when they come for you?"

—MANTRA FROM THE TV SHOW, *COPS*

Sure, it's easy to simply pop a worksheet, book chapter, or piece of music in the copy machine to pass along to friends or teachers. But are you breaking copyright law? Probably!

Know what copyright law is, and look for information about copyright when you're about to duplicate someone else's work in any form or format. Seek permission directly, or through a license if available.

"Fair use" takes into account how much is used and for what purposes. The line between "fair use" and copyright infringement isn't always clear. Although "nonprofit educational purposes" are among the factors considered, churches are not exempt.

And it's not just about pictures and written work. Showing movies in churches requires a public performance license. Church Video License (*www.cvil.com*) is a great source.

It has been reported that the author of a poem frequently read at funerals and graduations has sought thousands of dollars from churches involved in publishing her work without first buying a license from her.

Printer beware!

THE THREE-LEGGED STOOL OF EVALUATION

As Anglicans, we use the mantra of Richard Hooker (1555–1600) of "Scripture, tradition, and reason" as how we describe our polity in a nutshell. These areas can form a helpful framework for evaluating our educational mission and ministry.

- How are we teaching and using Scripture in our education and formation groups?
- How do we weave the history of the church, the hymns, symbols, liturgy, and stories into our classes and small groups?
- How do we encourage teachers and learners to employ human reason as they reflect on and state their beliefs?

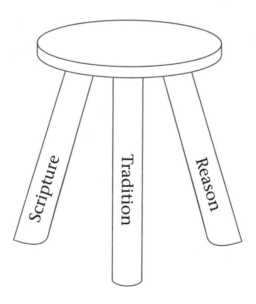

TEACHING TIPS

HOW TO HAVE A SUCCESSFUL CLASS

Shape an environment that supports learning and appropriate classroom behavior.

- All participants feel physically and emotionally safe.
- Group and individual behavioral problems are treated differently from each other.
- There are basic classroom routines.
- Energy is focused on students' strengths.
- The age group characteristics are known and there are appropriate expectations.
- Community is developed within the classroom.
- Discipline situations are opportunities for learning.
- Clearly defined guidelines are established that are appropriate to the age level and room (in positive terms).
- Everyone practices effective listening.
- Pro-social behavior is modeled by leaders.

Mix it up.

- Activities are eclectic, holistic, and experiential.
- A multitude of stimulating activities is offered.
- Choices are provided, depending on the nature of the class and participants.
- "Field trips" (sanctuary, sacristy, organ loft, food pantry, church garden, etc.) are taken.
- Time is allotted to finish projects!
- The story of God's people is related to our story today.

HOW TO TELL *THE* STORY

The Bible is a compilation of stories of God's people. It is about God's relationship with those who came before us and those who will come after us. It is our story today.

Throughout the ages, the storyteller has performed the important function of handing down society's traditions, history, and vision of life to each generation. The stories we hear play an important role in shaping our lives. Telling the story to others is what teaching and learning is all about.

Joseph Russell writes, "Our task is to celebrate and dramatize the story, to respond to it with music, visual form, word, and dance. We need to share the story for the sake of the story rather than using it to nail down a theological or moral truth."[1]

Suggested steps to prepare for sharing stories with children:

1. Read the story you want to tell.
2. Jot down on an index card the points and details that shape the story.
3. Imagine yourself telling the story, picturing it happening in your mind.
4. Repeat the process until you can actually see the scenes in your mind. Use the cards as prompts until you no longer need them.

---

1. Russell, Joseph P. *Sharing the Biblical Story* (Wilton, CT: Morehouse Barlow, 1979), 10.

JOHNNY'S ON THE CEILING

Is the noise level in your classroom above the safe decibel level? Are paper airplanes filtering out into the hall? Are the children speaking in tongues? No need to call the behavior police . . . assess what's going on first.

- **Look at the room:** Is it crowded? Too hot? Too cold? Chairs too big or small? Not enough ventilation or light?

- **Look at your schedule:** Are you crowding too many (or too few) activities in the time allotted? Is there a balance of experiential learning tapping into different learning styles?

- **Look at verbal communication:** Are you speaking all the time? Hope not! Is the vocabulary age-appropriate?

- **Look at non-verbal communication:** How is your facial expression and body language? What message are you sending?

- **Have you set classroom guidelines?** Work with participants to develop a set of classroom norms for behavior stated in positive terms.

- **Is one child the issue?** There may be a learning disability, physical or emotional issue, or other event in their life that is exhibiting itself in inappropriate behavior. Speak with the clergy and parents.

A well-prepared teacher has an engaged and successful learning environment.

WHEN SNAKES SHOW UP

Spring came early to St. Matthew's Episcopal Church in Wilton, Connecticut. The property committee had not had time to clean up the brush around the church building and the covers on the air conditioning units in the walls had not yet been removed.

While reading the week's Bible story to a full class of third graders, mostly boys, the teacher was wondering why everyone was watching her so intensely. Or were they looking beyond her at the wall?

Turning her head just as the children jumped up and began shrieking, she saw what they had been fixated upon. It would seem the warm weather had woken up the hibernating nest of garter snakes that had been living in the AC unit.

Were they looking for food or just enjoying hearing the story of Adam and Eve in the Garden of Eden?

Alas, the screaming sent the snakes back into the vent, and back into the woods. No one remembered the Bible story that day. And the property committee got to work the next day.

HOW WE LEARN

Children retain more when they're involved in the learning experience. The top of this cone depicts learning methods that utilize the learner's own experience. The bottom shows learning methods that rely on the experience of others. The learning methods are ranked from top to bottom, with the most effective methods at the top.

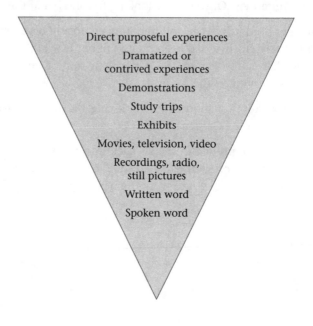

Direct purposeful experiences

Dramatized or contrived experiences

Demonstrations

Study trips

Exhibits

Movies, television, video

Recordings, radio, still pictures

Written word

Spoken word

THE BRAIN CREATED BY GOD

According to Dr. Howard Gardner, a psychologist and professor of neuroscience from Harvard University, human beings have nine different kinds of intelligence that reflect different ways of interacting with the world. When planning lessons, we need to keep our activities varied to tap into each person's potential.

Linguistic intelligence involves sensitivity to spoken and written language, the ability to learn languages, and the capacity to use language to accomplish certain goals.

Bodily/Kinesthetic intelligence is the capacity to use your whole body or parts of your body (your hands, your fingers, your arms) to solve a problem, make something, or put on some kind of production.

Spatial intelligence is the ability to represent the spatial world internally in your mind—the way a sailor or airplane pilot navigates the large spatial world, or the way a chess player or sculptor represents a more circumscribed spatial world.

Logical/Mathematical intelligence consists of the capacity to analyze problems logically, carry out mathematical operations, and investigate issues scientifically. It entails the ability to detect patterns, reason deductively, and think logically.

Musical/Rhythmic intelligence involves skill in the performance, composition, and appreciation of musical patterns.

Naturalist intelligence is the ability to discriminate among living things (plants, animals) and sensitivity to other features of the natural world (clouds, rock configurations).

Interpersonal intelligence is concerned with the capacity to understand the intentions, motivations, and desires of other people. It allows people to work effectively with others.

Intrapersonal intelligence entails the capacity to understand oneself, to appreciate one's feelings, fears, and motivations. It involves having an effective working model of us, and to be able to use such information to regulate our lives.

Existential intelligence is the ability and proclivity to pose (and ponder) questions about life, death, and ultimate realities.

AN INCLUSIVE CLASSROOM

Children (and youth and adults) who have learning differences are in all churches. As you integrate any child, especially one with learning differences, into regular classroom meetings, begin with who and where the child is, with her strengths, weaknesses, sensitivities, and abilities. As much as possible, draw this information from conversations with parents. What's most important is an ongoing relationship with the child, conversation with parents, lots of small steps, and trying one thing and then another, depending on what works as the child grows through different stages.

Be aware of including a range of learning possibilities in your teaching and lesson plans: group, individual, buddies; fine motor skills, larger motor skills; cognitive, imaginative; interactive, quiet; drama, craft, or music; and work stations, with different kinds of projects and materials.

The less unstructured time, the better. Unstructured, unplanned, empty time—time between activities, while some kids complete a task, or while others are going to the bathroom, leaving, or arriving—is more likely to cause anxiety or the need for redirection in children.

Remember that different children learn at different paces. Seek the child's strengths, while being aware of his or her limitations or growing edges. Seek help when needed.

WHO AM I?
A PRESCHOOLER!

If young (three-, four-, or five-year-old) children could describe themselves, here are some of the things they might tell us:

- The world is great and I'm starting to get a handle on it.
- I like unusual sounds, textures, smells, and sights.
- I like "experiments"—the messier, the better.
- I like being silly.
- Birthday parties are the best.
- I can dress myself, but I like someone to help me.
- There are scary changes in my life—starting school, meeting new people.
- I still want someone to take care of me, but I want to do lots of things by myself.
- I like games where everyone wins. Losing makes me cry.
- I love to run, tumble, hop, and jump.
- I might be able to count to ten and recognize my ABCs.
- My fine motor skills, like using scissors are still developing.
- I love to be read to—including stories from the Bible.
- I experience faith through my senses.
- I love to explore, test, observe, copy, imagine, and create.
- I thrive in a safe environment.
- God is love. Jesus is my friend. God is like my mommy or daddy.
- The Bible is a big book.
- My question: "What new thing is coming next?"

WHO AM I?
I'M SIX GOING ON EIGHT!

If young elementary age (six-, seven-, or eight-year-old) children could describe themselves, here are some of the things they might tell us:

- I love jokes and riddles!
- I have friends now. Sometimes it's because I like their toys, but sometimes it's because I'm happy to be with them.
- Sometimes I need an adult to help me figure out what is fair when playing with my friends.
- Bigger kids sometimes scare me. I like to feel "big" myself.
- I like knowing what is going to happen next.
- I like it when we begin with a prayer or song and end with a prayer! I like routines.
- I want to move around a lot.
- I'm learning to read and write better every day.
- I love to draw and create things—real and imaginary.
- I'm getting better at cutting, pasting, painting, and constructing things.
- I love stories about Jesus and people in the Bible.
- I want to participate in many things.
- God is Jesus' Father, a giver and a creator—a lot like magic. God has lots of power.
- The Bible is a big book of stories.
- My question: "Can I help?"

WHO AM I?
I'M THE BIG KID

If older elementary age (nine-, ten-, and eleven-year-old) children could describe themselves, they might tell us:

+ I'm trying to sort out what's true and what's not.
+ I want to feel that I'm good at things. I like to learn *how* to do something.
+ I have friends now and like to join groups to be with them like scouts and sports teams.
+ Rules and fairness matter to me. Usually my friends and I will figure out our own rules and might get upset if an adult tells us.
+ I'm not one of the little kids in school anymore.
+ I might get bored because I like to learn things on my own.
+ If you give me a choice, I will do what I like to do over and over and over again.
+ I can read and write, but might prefer art, music, or action instead.
+ God is powerful and can be a friend. God can also be like a judge—remember, rules are important to me!
+ The Bible is a big book of stories about Jesus and God, but is it true?
+ My question: What can I do?

WHO AM I?
I REALLY DON'T KNOW

If early adolescents (middle schoolers) could describe themselves, they might tell us:

* I'm trying to sort out my identity.
* I'm starting to separate from my parents and my family, turning to my peers for support.
* I may reject traditions and teachings I accepted as a child.
* Sometimes I'm painfully self-conscious. I lack self-confidence, can be awkward and self-critical.
* Emotionally, I can overreact, be moody, and unpredictable.
* Physically, I'm developing rapidly, leading to my incoordination and clumsiness.
* I make moral choices based on reciprocity.
* I've got loads of extra energy and physical activities help me burn it off.
* I need creative outlets to let me experiment—painting, writing, dance, music, service, cooking, sports . . .
* I need affirmation. I want to belong.
* I like ritual.
* I want all this God-stuff to be relevant to the things I struggle with every day: loneliness, anger, sexuality, fear . . .
* I'm looking for guidance, clear limits, and guidelines.
* I want to contribute. Ask me!
* God is a spirit, mystery and Savior.
* The Bible is a manual to live by.
* My question: Who am I?

WHO AM I?
I'M WORKING ON IT

If older adolescents (high schoolers) could describe themselves, they might tell us:

- I'm forging my own identity, struggling to "be real," to be myself, including my gender identity.
- I'm separating from my parents and family, finding support among my peers.
- I'm starting to accept some of the beliefs and traditions that I rejected only a few years ago.
- Asking tough spiritual questions helps my faith to grow.
- I ask lots of questions (in my head, if not aloud), and canned answers don't cut it.
- If you expect me to listen to you, be authentic and don't pretend to know what you don't know.
- Be willing to wrestle with me over what's really important in life and faith.
- I am stressed. I may be juggling a job along with a ton of schoolwork. I may be worried about college and my future. I need a safe place to decompress.
- As I finish high school I'm starting to make moral decisions based on what's best for everyone, not just my friends.
- Physically, I'm transitioning into full adulthood, but my emotions and experiences might not match my physical development and strength.
- Model for me what it means to be a growing Christian.
- God is in tension between "man," Jesus, and a universal God.
- The Bible is a summary of values and truths.
- My questions: Who am I? Where do I fit in the world?

A ROOMFUL
OF HOMER SIMPSONS

Believe it or not, adults in your congregation do want to learn. They just don't want to go to Sunday school. They are hungry for assistance and support in putting their faith into action in the world outside of the church—at work, at home, and in the community.

Today's adults:

- are experienced;
- are independent;
- have established values, beliefs, and opinions;
- have a deep need to be self-directing;
- tend to have a problem-centered orientation to learning;
- look for practical consequences;
- want to be respected;
- are relatively mature and responsible;
- participate for many reasons;
- expect physical comfort;
- may not always attend;
- sometimes resist change—really!

There's a "life cycle" of adult Christian formation in which all adults fit into one of these categories. They also move in and out of each phase, depending on their life circumstances:

- *Phase 1:* Searching—"I'm looking for something . . ."
- *Phase 2:* Commitment—"Okay, I'm in, now what?"
- *Phase 3:* Commissioning—"I'm ready for leadership."
- *Phase X:* Recovery/Re-Entry—"I'm back."

This last phase can be repeated over and over again and occur during any of these phases.

NOAH GATHERED THEM TWO BY TWO

God had a plan when he told Noah to gather two of every creature. There is security and camaraderie in team teaching. Two adults per class is an especially good model for Safe Church practices and allows someone always to be ready to attend to a specific child's immediate needs should something occur while the other attends to the lesson with the other children.

One team teacher can guide the class while the other observes and assists. Both can alternate roles during a session or from week to week. Participants get to know two adults for the price of one and each adult is able to teach from their strengths (like art or music) while allowing their partner to focus on their strengths (like story-telling or organization).

Many volunteers find it difficult to commit to a full year of teaching. Build a team of teachers per class so that each takes a month, one Sunday a month, or one Sunday a quarter. Follow the same strategy if you have a mid-week program, too. Make sure they are all present together from time to time to reassure the class they are not being tag-teamed, never knowing who will be their teacher each week. Following a pattern is important.

Be flexible in combining any of these models. You might have teams that teach for a full year or that are assigned for only a quarter or season. The younger the child, the more important it is to have the same adult with them each Sunday. Create a model that works for your church and your children.

PRAYERS TO
AND FOR CHILDREN

A CHILDREN'S CREED

I believe in God above,
I believe in Jesus' love,
I believe His Spirit, too
comes to show me what to do.
I believe that I can be
kind and gentle, Lord like thee.

A BIRTHDAY PRAYER

O God, our times are in your hand: Look with favor, we pray,
on your child, [name] as *she* begins another year. Grant that *she*
may grow in wisdom and grace, and strengthen *her* trust in your
goodness all the days of *her* life; through Jesus Christ our Lord.
Amen.

DAILY PRAYER

Bless us as we come to grow,
And teach us things we need to know.
Help us love one another as we love You.
And let us serve You
Each day in all that we do.

WHEN TO SAY WHEN GRANDMA OR FIDO DIES

- **Discuss death naturally before it occurs.** Death is a time when the "you" (the part that laughs when you are happy and cries when you are sad) leaves the body. We sometimes call this part our soul.
- **Recognize God's plan for cycles.** Use seeds, flower bulbs, and the life cycle of a butterfly as conversational springboards.
- **Share sorrow, even with children.** If a pet dies and a child asks questions about whether the pet will go to heaven, say you don't know, but you know God has a plan. It's okay to be unsure, because we trust God.
- **Stress a child's own security and your continuing love and concern for the child or adult.** "We don't turn off love when someone dies."
- **Share happy memories.** Help children write stories of good times shared with the person who died. Look at photographs together and tell stories.
- **Include children in grief.** Cry openly in appropriate ways. Give extra security. They will learn from your expressions of grief and compassion.
- **Continue routines and rituals.** Play. Draw. Pray. Sing. Share stories of God's love. Share a meal together.
- **Encourage questions.** Express your belief, but you don't need to have answers.
- **Reassure children that they are safe and loved.** Some of their fear is that others they love will die and leave them. Recognize that there are many who are still are present for them.

HOW TO GET PAINT OUT OF AN EASTER DRESS

Some children come to church dressed in school clothes or play clothes. Some come dressed in their "Sunday best." After all, it is Sunday! Of course, it's usually the little princess with the lacey white dress who refuses to wear a smock and chooses to paint her sleeves instead of the paper you've put in front of her.

Homemade Washable Paint

- ¾ cup liquid tempera paint
- ¼ cup liquid detergent (Ivory Snow or Dreft Liquid)

Combine and stir well. Easily washes out of most fabrics.

Easy Watercolors

Don't throw out those old, dried-out markers. Let the children dip them in water and use them like watercolors. When the tip turns white, then it's time to throw them away!

Sidewalk Paint

- ¼ cup cornstarch
- ¼ cup water
- 6–8 drops of food coloring

Mix cornstarch and cold water together. Add food coloring and stir. Repeat to make different colors. This paint can be easily washed off with water and is great for painting large areas temporarily!

WHAT SHOULD BE IN YOUR CLASSROOM?

Preschool and Kindergarten

- child-size table and chairs
- space for movement, play, and story time
- easy to clean carpeting
- dress up clothes
- washable dolls and stuffed animals
- blocks
- art supplies
- picture books
- CD player with appropriate music CDs for small children

Elementary (First through Fifth Grade)

- appropriately sized table and chairs
- space for movement and drama
- children's Bibles
- prayer books (BCP) and Hymnals
- art supplies
- wall space for posters, artwork, timelines, etc.

Youth (Middle and High Schools)

- seating—tables and chairs may not be necessary
- at least one table for supplies and any activity if needed
- art supplies, including magazines and current newspapers
- Bibles, BCPs, and Hymnals
- reference books and maps (if your space is not "wired")
- newsprint and markers or whiteboards
- electronic equipment as needed

HOW TO MINISTER TO BULLIES

Bullying among children is significantly rising in the United States. Children lacking spiritual and moral definition find bullying an effective tool for getting what they want. It happens every day at schools, in neighborhoods—even at church. How do we minister to everyone yet make kids feel safe? Can we make a difference in just a few hours a week?

- **Teach frequently on the Golden Rule.** It seems so simplistic, but to these kids, the Golden Rule is a great revelation. How freeing it is for children when they understand that yelling and bullying aren't what God had in mind for them. Involve "bullies" in role-playing the biblical stories.

- **Pull bullies close.** Bullies need lots of love because bullying is based on fear. Make it a point to include a child labeled as a bully. Break down barriers with Christian love and keep the child close so you can monitor his behavior.

- **Correct, don't challenge.** When correction becomes necessary, and it will, make sure you do it the right way. For younger children, stoop down to their eye level; get on your knees to have a chat. Don't embarrass, humiliate, or make a public spectacle of the child.

- **Take threats seriously.** If you are threatened or another child is threatened take the threat seriously. Quickly separate the bully from the other child and immediate take the child to your clergy. Take threats seriously so children will know that making threats won't be tolerated in your ministry.

Every child that bullies needs love and attention, but unfortunately, some children won't be willing to change their behaviors, at least not for a long while. Be patient but don't neglect the other children in your ministry. Don't forget to pray for the children in your care. Prayer can move mountains.

The Golden Rule

In everything do to others as you would have them do to you;
for this is the law and the prophets. (Matthew 7:12)

Love for Enemies

But I say to you that listen, Love your enemies, do good to those
who hate you, bless those who curse you, pray for those who
abuse you. If anyone strikes you on the cheek, offer the other
also; and from anyone who takes away your coat do not with-
hold even your shirt. Give to everyone who begs from you; and
if anyone takes away your goods, do not ask for them again. Do
to others as you would have them do to you. (Luke 6:27–31)

HOW TO LEAD QUICK GAMES

Whether to begin a class, get the wiggles out, or fill up some remaining time, it is always good to have a few tricks up your sleeve or ready-to-go ideas in your back pocket.

Name Roll—toss a ball of yarn to students, each holding on to the yarn as it is tossed to the next person. Name a Bible person, vocabulary word, etc.

Scrabble Scramble—write out the alphabet on index cards (one letter per card, two of the letters A-H-N-S-T, three of E-O). Distribute. Name or describe a biblical character—all must scramble to spell it out.

"That's Me!"—When something is named that describes you, jump up and shout, "That's me!" and then sit down again. Place close attention and you will learn a lot about each other.

"Color Prayer"—Pass out colored sheets of paper. Name the color and whoever has that paper prays for something (i.e.: red—apple).

"What's Different?"—In groups of two, each person looks at the other. Sit back to back and change one thing about yourself (unbutton a button, untie a shoe). Turn around and face each other. Each one guesses what has changed in the other. Then say, "Let's change back to the lesson and see how it can change our lives!"

I HAVE TO LEAD
AN ADULT STUDY?

Planning for an adult class can be collaborative, with class members taking responsibility as well as the leader. Leadership can be shared, rotating from one member to another each week. Experiential methods can help adults expand their learning, while group discussion generally proves to be the method that generates the most energy.

An adult group leader can encourage candid discussion in the following ways:

+ Maintain an atmosphere of freedom and inquiry.
+ Keep a sense of humor.
+ Offer genuine appreciation for the ideas and feelings expressed.
+ Accept differences of opinion, affirming participants, helping to explore new ideas.
+ Welcome silent spaces, giving everyone time to think and/or the courage to speak.
+ Have an air horn available to interrupt those who dominate the conversation or fail to make their point within three minutes.
+ Break into smaller groups for part of the discussion.
+ Provide chocolate or cookies and good coffee.

WHAT ADULTS SHOULD BE TALKING ABOUT

What topics are adults interested in for study? First, it needs to be relevant to their personal life wherever they may be on their journey of faith as well as phase of life. Second, small groups that are scheduled at convenient times and that only require a commitment of less than six weeks. Bring in speakers, read a book together, discuss the intersection of faith with the news, support parents. Most importantly, have a facilitator who knows how to facilitate (not necessarily a "sage on the stage") and make sure the group develops a set of norms for inclusive and fair conversation.

aging	spirituality
Baptism	stress
Bible	pop theology (movies)
crime/violence	worship
death	parenting
faith in the workplace	caring for parents
human rights	the prayer book
denominations	social justice
health and wholeness	hymnology
life management	Christian heroes and heroines
marriage	Sabbath
mission	stewardship
environmental issues	contemporary saints
prayer	interfaith issues
sexuality	

PARTIERS, BIBLE THUMPERS, OR DO-GOODERS?

In addition to the generation into which they were born (and thus how they learned how to learn) adults can also be grouped into interest areas.

Fellowship—This group is all about the socializing and informal discussions with topics that are relevant today. Relationships are key.

Traditionalist—A breed that is after being imparted with wisdom from the expert. They enjoy lectures and following a set curriculum.

Neo-traditionalist—Those folks who have returned to church after a hiatus and only remember what education used to be; they are seeking something new—but not too new.

Social Action—Faith tends to be a private matter, but put a hammer in their hands or stand up for a justice issue, and they'll be right there on the picket line with you.

Combos—Any mix of the above categories.

Party-Timers—These are very similar to the Fellowship group. Mix in some wine and cheese along with entertainment, and you've got a captive audience. Subliminal education can take place through interactive centerpieces and fortune cookies stuffed with scripture passages.

IS THIS THE RIGHT QUESTION?

Jesus wanted people to think. In Matthew, Jesus is a teacher who opened the scriptures. Even if you are not a biblical scholar, just teaching children how to ask questions and that it is all right to ask is a tremendous accomplishment. You will learn also! Encourage creative thinking by asking the right question.

Ask open-ended questions.

- For example, instead of "Where was Jesus born?" ask "Why do you think God allowed Jesus to be born in a manger in a stable?" or
- "If Jesus was born today, what kind of place would God choose? Why?"

Ask follow-up questions.

- What do you mean by . . . ?
- What reasons do you have?
- How did you decide . . . ?
- Tell me more about . . .

Wait for the answers.

- Establish "think time"—a few moments of silence for students to think about the question, for shy participants to muster the courage to respond, for those who are bolder to decide to risk their answers or dominate the conversation.
- Have students write their answers first.
- Wait until most have thought of a response before letting anyone answer.

Don't evaluate discussion responses.

Discussion is just that—discussion. To encourage all to talk, their responses should not be judged. In order to affirm everyone in a class discussion, offer a summary of what you've heard around the table or room. It forces you (and everyone) to pay attention and it's a way to check in and make sure the opinion given has been understood.

Encourage questions.

Yes, yes, yes! They're not interruptions, but "teachable moments." Every question is valid and important. Modeling imaginative questions brings about more questions.

"Chills and Kills" vs. "Sparks and Embarks"

- ◆ "Yes" or "no" questions chill conversation.
- ◆ "Why" questions open up conversations.

HOW TO LEAD A BOOK DISCUSSION GROUP

Study groups are an opportunity for participants to discover and struggle with ideas and to learn something new. The content of the study book is certainly important, but the spirit with which the book is discussed is even more so. Within a prayerful, open environment that promotes discussion in a challenging but affirming way, there is the opportunity for spiritual growth and faith formation.

One member of the group can facilitate all the sessions. Or rotating facilitation can be used, in which several or all participants share the task. The facilitator does not need to be an expert on the subject of the book. The facilitator does need to read the material for the session and come prepared to help the group grapple with its central ideas.

Discussion starters:

- Did anything surprise, excite, confuse, anger, or upset you?
- What questions or concerns does the text raise in your mind?
- In what ways does what the author is saying relate to your experience?
- How does the text support or affirm your faith?
- How does the text challenge your faith?
- What faith questions does it raise for you?
- Has the text stirred you to some form of action? If so, what?

DERAILMENTS AND DOMINATORS

The role of a facilitator is not to have all the answers, but to provide an environment for a successful gathering.

Tips to be a successful facilitator:

- Arrive early and prepare the room. Arrange chairs, post newsprint, distribute agendas or materials.
- Greet everyone as they arrive.
- Start on time and end on time.
- Begin and end with prayer.

From time to time you will face a group that has a member or two that disturbs the flow and plan of a class or meeting. That calls for a more active role as a facilitator:

- **Someone dominates the discussion.** Suggest adding their concern to a piece of newsprint for later conversation.
- **The group gets off track.** Refocus the group by restating the question, issue at hand, or agenda item.
- **Not everyone is participating.** Invite those who have not spoken by name if they have anything they would like to add. Ask if everyone has had an opportunity to speak before moving on to another topic.
- **Group members argue with one another.** Ask for a brief moment of silence. Then ask each member of the group to list a pro and a con about the topic. Review group norms if necessary.

PAPERWORK
AND CHECKLISTS

AN INVITATION TO SERVE

Develop an easy checklist for inviting adults (or teens) to serve the Body of Christ through your Christian education or youth ministry.

Supporting Ministries

I would be willing to help by:

- ☐ praying regularly for leaders and learners
- ☐ assisting with publicity
- ☐ taking charge of the supply closet
- ☐ contributing craft materials
- ☐ taking charge of refreshments for younger children
- ☐ providing refreshments for a group for a month
- ☐ purchasing a book or resource for a class
- ☐ contributing toward the cost of the curriculum
- ☐ keeping weekly records
- ☐ providing transportation when needed
- ☐ being a chaperone when needed

Teaching Ministries

I would be willing to help by:

- ☐ being a coordinator for the _____ age
- ☐ leading the _____ group
  - ○ for the _____ season
  - ○ for the year
- ☐ assisting a leader in the _____ group
  - ○ for the _____ season
  - ○ for the year
- ☐ being a substitute when needed

A COVENANT WITH TEACHERS AND LEADERS

As a teacher, you can expect the church and its leadership to provide:

- a supportive congregation
- curriculum materials
- training experiences
- leadership and resource persons
- supplies and materials that are helpful to the teaching experience
- a clean, well-lit, furnished room or gathering space
- support from clergy and lay leaders
- opportunities (including financial assistance) to grow in one's own Christian faith

Our church and its leadership expects our volunteer teachers to:

- spend time on preparation for each class session
- arrive at least fifteen minutes before a session begins
- attend worship
- get to know and plan for ways to meet the needs of each person in their class
- be willing to show and share their own faith
- be willing to promote the Episcopal Church's theology based on scripture, tradition, and reason
- grow in faith by attending training and study events

RECIPE FOR A CHURCH SCHOOL LESSON

Early in the Week (*Sunday or Monday*)

- **Read** through the lesson plan (fifteen to twenty minutes).
- **Write** the teaching object or the purpose of the lesson on a 3" x 5" card.
- **Post** the card where you can see it daily (bathroom mirror, refrigerator).
- **Think/meditate** on the meaning of this concept in your life and worship.
- Put all this info "on the back burner" and let it **"simmer."**

Midweek (*Monday through Thursday*)

- **Simmer.**
- **Gather** info and ideas as the week progresses, picking up items that will be needed or calling the church to request supplies.
- **Listen** to the news, music, movies, and TV shows—where do you hear the week's concept?

End of the Week (*Friday and Saturday*)

- **Plan** to teach (this is your major planning session; allow enough time).
- **Read** and visualize the lesson plan in action ("see" each step with the children in your learning space).
- **Make notes** in your teacher's guide or lesson planning sheet.
- **Review** it again, focusing on you, the teacher:
    - Are you interested in the lesson?
    - Does each activity flow easily from the last?
    - What will you see that will tell you that the children are learning?
    - What is your prayer for the children and this lesson this week?

Sunday

- **Arrive** fifteen to twenty minutes early to arrange your classroom.
- **Prepare** your classroom—gather any needed supplies, put out a "start up" activity for "early birds."
- **Teach** the lesson.
- **Evaluate** the lesson later in the day. Learn from your experience in planning for the next week.

If the lesson is looked at for the first time on Saturday night (not to mention Sunday morning), the necessary supplies will not be ready and you may choose the easiest (and probably quickest and least engaging) activity. This may not be the best for your class, in which you will then have a class of eager but bored children!

LESSON PLAN TEMPLATE

Theme: _____

Date: _____

My goal for this session is:

Checklist of things to include in my blocks of time for this lesson:

_____ Early/first to arrive activities

_____ Introduce the theme

_____ Opening prayer

_____ Learning activities

      ○ verbal/linguistic

      ○ musical

      ○ visual/spatial

      ○ interpersonal

      ○ intrapersonal

      ○ bodily/kinesthetic

      ○ logical/mathematical

      ○ naturalist

      ○ spiritual

_____ closing prayer

Block One Activity: _____ (____ minutes)

Block Two Activity: _____ (____ minutes)

Block Three Activity: _____ (____ minutes)

Block Four Activity: _____ (____ minutes)

Block Five Activity: _____ (____ minutes)

Supplies needed:

Evaluation thoughts: What worked well? What didn't work?

THE SUPPLY CLOSET

All of these can be put into labeled plastic clear containers or shoeboxes.

aluminum foil

art foam

baby food jars

baby oil

baggies

balloons

balls (all sorts)

beads

beanbags

bed sheet (for floor)

birdseed

burlap

butcher paper rolls

buttons

candles (votive, pillar)

cardboard sheets

cardboard tubes

cartons (milk, egg)

catalogs

CD player

chalk

chenille wires

clay/Play-doh

clothespins

coffee cans

coffee filters

confetti

construction paper

cookie cutters

cotton balls

craft sticks

crayons

crepe paper streamers

envelopes

extension cords

fabric scraps

felt

flowers (plastic, silk)

foil pie tins

food coloring

foreign coins

glitter

glue (bottles, sticks)

hole punches (hand held)

index cards

jingle bells

magazines

magnet strips

magnifying glasses

markers

measuring sticks

muffin cups

nature items

newspaper

notebook paper

oatmeal containers

origami paper

costumes/bathrobes

paints of all kinds

paint smocks (shirts)

paintbrushes

painter's tape

paper bags

paper clips and fasteners

pasta shapes

pastels

pencils (colored and lead)

picture file

pinecones

pipe cleaners

poster board

puppets

raffia

resealable bags

rhythm instruments

ribbon (curling)

rope

rubber bands

rulers

safety pins

salt

sandpaper

scarves

scissors (adult and child)

scratch paper

seeds and beans (a variety)

sequins

shells

shoeboxes

sponges (cut in shapes)

stamps and stamp pads

staplers and staples

starch

stickers

strawberry baskets

straws

string

tablecloths (plastic)

tape (scotch and masking)

thumbtacks

tissue paper

toothpicks

trim (rick-rack)

twine

utensils (plastic)

wallpaper samples

wax paper

wiggle eyes

wire hangers

yarn

CHECKLIST OF NECESSARY NURSERY SUPPLIES

- [ ] disposable diapers
- [ ] paper lining for changing tables
- [ ] pre-moistened wipes
- [ ] tissues
- [ ] cotton balls
- [ ] first-aid kit with syrup of ipecac, thermometer, alcohol/antibiotic ointment, bandages, cold pack
- [ ] name tags and markers
- [ ] plastic bags and ties for soiled clothes
- [ ] disinfectants and nontoxic cleaning solutions
- [ ] paper towels
- [ ] electric outlet covers
- [ ] emergency manual
- [ ] posted fire exit plans/maps
- [ ] children's books and toys
- [ ] nursery pager system (if a large congregation)
- [ ] telephone
- [ ] fire extinguishers
- [ ] smoke and carbon monoxide detectors (check batteries often and replace twice a year)
- [ ] rocking chairs
- [ ] child-size table and chairs
- [ ] cribs
- [ ] changing table(s)
- [ ] lockable cabinet for supplies
- [ ] hooks for hanging coats and diaper bags

AN EMERGENCY PLAN

Every church needs an emergency plan, whether for fire, natural disaster, or something completely unpredictable. There's nothing like realizing you need to evacuate thirty preschoolers when an alarm unexpectedly goes off during worship. Develop a plan and post it in all classrooms, bathrooms, and stairwells.

Consider these questions:

- What sort of fire alarms do you have? Can they be heard everywhere?
- Do rooms have signs posted pointing to the nearest exit?
- Where is the prearranged meeting place to gather outside of the building?
- The teachers in classrooms with small children cannot evacuate all of the children alone. Who can get to the nursery easily to help?
- During worship, who will be responsible to check on rooms where others may be?
- What is the signal that it is safe to reenter?

Tips:

- Tie knots every two feet in a long rope (clothesline) to be used by small children to keep them in a line for an orderly exit. (Great for nature walks, too!)
- Duplicate the floor plan of your building/s and mark off primary and alternate routes for each room in case of emergencies.
- Practice a fire drill with your congregation several times a year.

WHERE TO PUT
THE FIRST AID KIT

Medical incidents occur all the time at church from children scraping their knees and needing a band aid to an elderly person having heart problems. There are several places in the church to consider having a kit: the church office, near the Nursery and classrooms, the gym or fellowship hall, and in the bus or van if your church has one.

A good first aid kit includes:

- Band-Aids (all sizes)
- antibiotic ointment
- disinfectant spray
- gauze wrap (Kerlix or Kling), muslin swath, safety pins
- scissors
- tape
- gloves
- alcohol wipes
- disposable instant cold packs

If you have a health care professional in your congregation, ask his or her assistance. If you keep any medications in your kit, make sure they are locked. And keep all of these out of range of small children. Post signage around your building stating the location of first aid areas, along with reminders to call 9-1-1. Many churches now have automated external defibrillators (AED).

Check out the Episcopal Church's Health Ministries Network for lots of health information (*http://www.episcopalhealthministries.org*).

A SANDWICH EVALUATION

Delia Halverson, a United Methodist Church educator, has developed a clever process for evaluation. Balance recommendations with commendations. She states, "With a balanced diet, we grow in our ministry to Christ and the church."

Begin with the bottom slice of bread and work your way up in building your sandwich.

7. Olive—Top it off with a least one area to improve in the next session.

6. Bread—Offer another commendation to hold the evaluation together.

5. Pickles—Let's talk about when we had a pickle of a problem.

4. Lettuce—Let us rejoice over a particularly good experience.

3. Meat—What are some recommendations for change?

2. Cheese—What are some concerns that became apparent?

1. Bread—Evaluations need to begin with some commendations. What was good?

CURRICULUM EVALUATION WORKSHEET

Title of resource: _____

Publisher: _____

Age level: _____ Number of sessions: _____

☐ Dated ☐ Undated

Rating Scale: 1 = Strong ——————— 5 = Weak

☐ Clear objectives support the goals of our education program.

☐ The beliefs, vocabulary, examples are compatible with the Episcopal faith.

☐ Scripture is presented without offering personal interpretation.

☐ Biblical themes (creation, sin, judgment, reconciliation, redemption) are developed age-appropriately.

☐ Balance of Old Testament, Gospels, and New Testament is acceptable.

☐ Baptism, Eucharist, and Episcopal content is offered.

☐ Activities support individuals putting concepts into action, including social issues and personal behavior.

☐ Material is age–appropriate.

☐ Teaching plan is easy to use.

☐ There are a variety of learning activities.

☐ Material is culturally relevant to audience.

☐ A home-use component is available.

☐ Art and graphics are appropriate to lesson.

☐ Supplementary material is needed to implement.

☐ Cost is within budget.

HOW TO GET INPUT FROM TEACHERS

It is helpful to check in with teachers from time to time, too. These questions can be asked formerly on a handout, via e-mail survey, at a teachers' meeting, or in one-on-one conversation.

I volunteer in the church school because:

One thing I have learned from a recent lesson I taught:

Parts of my class sessions that children respond to best are when:

Times when I feel I am losing the children's attention is when:

How much time do you spend in preparation?

Do you have enough materials and ideas to choose from?

What would you like to add to the curriculum?

What three things do you find most rewarding?

What three things do you find most challenging?

HOW TO GET INPUT FROM PARENTS

It is helpful to check in with parents from time to time. These questions can be asked formerly on a handout, via e-mail survey, or in one-on-one conversation.

What do you want for your children from our Christian education programs?

Does the church school's curriculum meet your needs? Explain:

Do your children enjoy church school? How do you know?

From what each of your children tell you about church school, do you know the stories or themes they are learning?

Rank these aspects of church school in order of importance.
(5=most, 1=least)

Being with peers	1	2	3	4	5
Bible stories	1	2	3	4	5
Relation of faith to daily living	1	2	3	4	5
Teacher/child relationships	1	2	3	4	5

What are some of the tough religious questions your children have asked?

How can we support you in nurturing your child's faith?

REGISTRATION FORMS

_____

First   Middle   Last

_____

Address

_____

City   State   Zip

_____

Parent/guardian

_____

Parent/guardian

Name preferred by child: _____

Date of birth: / /   Grade: _____

Allergies or health alerts:

Learning strengths or weaknesses:

Names and ages of siblings:

☐ I give permission for my child's photograph to be used for
   church purposes in newsletters, newspapers, and social media,
   including the church's website, knowing their name will not
   be associated with any photograph.

☐ Only the following persons have my permission to pick up my
   child from the classroom or an event:

   ○ Name/relationship:

   ○ Name/relationship:

   ○ Name/relationship:

Emergency phone numbers:

_____

#:   Name/relationship

_____

#:   Name/relationship

_____

Signature of parent or legal guardian   Date

THE DREADED PERMISSION SLIP

Check with your local legal advisors before finalizing any permission slips. Your diocese, insurance company or local regulations may determine the wording. Handing them out is easy. The trick is getting them turned in.

Sample Permission Slip

I hereby give permission for _____ to participate in _____ (field trip/retreat) as planned by _____ Church. It is my understanding that only authorized vehicles and drivers will be used. I understand that the church has insurance coverage with this trip. I also give permission for my child to be included in any pictures in connection to this program.

_____

Child's name (print)

_____

Parent or legal guardian's name (print)

_____

Emergency cell phone

_____

Alternate phone   Name/relationship to child

_____

Signature of parent or legal guardian   Date

MEDIA RELEASE

Media Release

On behalf of my child, the undersigned parent does agree to grant to _____, permission to record on film, videotape, or audiotape, the participation of the minor child. The undersigned parent/guardian further agrees that any or all of the material recorded may be used, in any form, as part of any future productions made by the _____ and further, that such use shall be without payment of fees, royalties, special credit, or other compensation to or for the benefit of minor child, parent, or any other person or entity.

_____
Signature of parent or legal guardian   Date

A COVENANT FOR A MISSION TRIP

On the mission trip, I understand that I need to agree to some conditions. As a member of the mission trip, I also represent my church and will do my best to represent it well. While my parents may not be with me, I will listen and follow the adults who serve as our leaders.

I agree:

- to be grateful for this opportunity to serve others;
- to show respect toward those we meet;
- to show respect for others on the mission trip;
- that I need to respect the privacy of persons and property;
- that if I have a disagreement, I will take it to an adult leader;
- to listen to the adults leaders and follow their instructions;
- to agree to the tasks we are given without complaint;
- to keep a positive attitude;
- to help with meals and clean up;
- to leave electronics at home (or give them to an adult leader);
- to let an adult know if I need help;
- I will do this by being kind, avoiding negative language, helping others when they need it, pitching in whenever possible.

I will follow these guidelines. If I have difficulty following them, I understand the adult leaders will talk with me about this. I understand that violation of this covenant may cause me to be sent home at my own expense.

_____

Name   Signature   Date

As the parent/guardian, I have reviewed this covenant with my child.

_____

Signature of parent or legal guardian   Date

Thanks to Maureen Hagen for permission to share this.

THE BUDGET

Office Expenses: TOTAL: _____
  Supplies   _____
  Postage   _____
  Computer   _____

Programs: TOTAL: _____
  Curriculum
      Children   _____
      Youth   _____
      Adult   _____
  Nursery/Child Care   _____
  Vacation Bible School   _____
  Confirmation   _____
  Baptismal Preparation   _____
  Family/Intergenerational   _____
  Seasonal (Lent, Advent)   _____

Celebrations and Special Events: TOTAL: _____
  Christmas Pageant   _____
  Gifts (graduation, etc.)   _____
  Celebrations   _____
  Speakers   _____

Leadership Development: TOTAL: _____
  Dues and Subscriptions   _____
  Teacher Training   _____
  Workshops   _____

                                            TOTAL: _____

THE ANNUAL REPORT

In January every year many of us tune into the State of the Union address given by the President of the United States. While not quite the same as rising to "Hail to the Chief," congregations hold an annual meeting to elect new vestry members, see the budget for the year to come, and discuss the mission and ministry of the church.

You will most likely be asked to submit an Annual Report for your area of oversight. Don't panic. Follow this simple formula. To make it easier in the long run, keep track of all this stuff throughout the year. Passing the info along to the Vestry each month will inform them of all the great things you do all year long.

- Stats: (you'll need this for the parochial report, too)
    - Number of children registered
    - Number of youth registered
    - Average church school attendance
    - Number of teachers and volunteers
    - Number of baptisms
    - Number of confirmations
    - Number of new families
- Goals from the previous year
- Accomplishments:
    - Events and programs
    - Curriculum used
- Goals for the coming year
- Warm fuzzies (comments and thanks)

PRAYERS TO BEGIN MEETINGS OR THE CONSUMPTION OF FOOD

Almighty and everliving God, ruler of all things in heaven and earth, hear our prayers for this parish family. Strengthen the faithful, arouse the careless, and restore the penitent. Grant us all things necessary for our common life, and bring us all to be of one heart and mind within your holy Church; through Jesus Christ our Lord. Amen. (BCP p. 817)

Give ear, O my people, to my teaching; incline your ears to the words of my mouth. I will open my mouth in a parable; I will utter dark sayings from old, things that we have heard and known, that our ancestors have told us. We will not hide them from their children; we will tell to the coming generation the glorious deeds of the Lord, and his might, and the wonders he has done. Amen. (Psalm 78:1–4)

Blessed are you, O Lord God, King of the Universe, for you give us food to sustain our lives and make our hearts glad; through Jesus Christ our Lord. Amen. (BCP p. 835)

O God of goodness, bless this table and those planted around, like an orchard growing in the garden of life. As our bodies delight in the fruits of your earth, may our lives flow with goodness like a mighty river. Amen. (Based on Psalm 1:3)

EPISCOPAL STUFF

WHAT IS THE EPISCOPAL CHURCH?

As Episcopalians, we are followers of Jesus Christ, our Lord, and we believe in the Father, Son, and Holy Spirit. We are part of the Anglican Communion, an inheritor of two thousand years of catholic and apostolic tradition dating from Christ himself.

The Episcopal Church came into existence as an independent denomination after the American Revolution, rooted in the Church of England. Today it has almost three million members in 110 dioceses across the United States, Europe, the Caribbean, and Central and South America.

Bishops in the Episcopal Church are elected by individual dioceses and are consecrated into the apostolic succession, considered to witness to an unbroken line of church leadership beginning with the apostles themselves. Any man or woman is eligible for ordination as a deacon, priest, or bishop. Lay people exercise a vital role in the governance and ministry of our church.

Our liturgy retains ancient structure and traditions and is celebrated in many languages. We consider the Bible to be divinely inspired, and hold the Eucharist to be the central act of Christian worship within the Book of Common Prayer. All baptized Christians are welcome to receive Holy Communion, no matter their age. We believe in amendment of life, the forgiveness of sin, and life everlasting.

WHAT IS THE ANGLICAN COMMUNION?

The Episcopal Church is one of forty-four national and regional church associations in 166 countries worldwide that make up the Anglican Communion. We're more than eighty million members strong (and growing), a rather loosely based confederation held together by Jesus Christ and the distinctive beliefs we share. These are based on the principles of the English Reformation, episcopal government by apostolic succession, a liturgical worship style, and the Bible informed and interpreted by tradition and reason.

Our spiritual leader is the Archbishop of Canterbury. His headquarters is at Lambeth Palace in London, England. The archbishop is not a pope; he makes no claims to infallibility, and his formal authority is limited to England. Nonetheless, he is considered a spiritual leader and Episcopalians accord him high respect.

The Anglican Communion is the third-largest body of Christians in the world. This means that practically anywhere you go you'll find a church that worships nearly the same way Episcopalians do. All of these churches have prayer books, though they are often written and adopted by each local body, adding a richness and distinction reflective of the home culture. Members of one church can easily transfer membership to another, regardless of the country (or continent). Joining the Episcopal Church automatically makes you a member of the Anglican Communion.

PROVINCES OF THE EPISCOPAL CHURCH

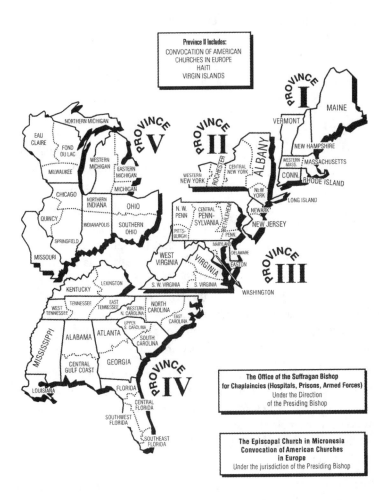

Province II Includes:
CONVOCATION OF AMERICAN
CHURCHES IN EUROPE
HAITI
VIRGIN ISLANDS

The Office of the Suffragan Bishop
for Chaplaincies (Hospitals, Prisons, Armed Forces)
Under the Direction
of the Presiding Bishop

The Episcopal Church in Micronesia
Convocation of American Churches
in Europe
Under the jurisdiction of the Presiding Bishop

HOW TO USE THREE-LEGGED STOOLS

Just like dairy farmers.

Of course, Episcopalians use three-legged stools to sit firmly and securely while we go about our work. However, we also use the three-legged stool as a metaphor for the way we define authority in the Episcopal Church.

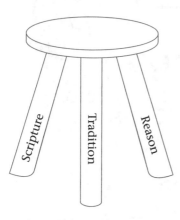

The three legs are the Bible, tradition, and reason, in this order. Holy Scripture is paramount as a way of defining what we believe and how we believe it. Does that mean we take the Bible literally? Not usually, though we do take it seriously.

When Episcopalians talk about tradition, we are referring to the many ways that the saints before us have dealt with issues of faith and doctrine. Let's face it, there are many modern concerns upon which the Bible is more or less silent, like nuclear warfare and premarital sex, so we consult the thoughts and writings of pious ancestors in the tradition to help us make a way forward.

The third leg is reason. By this we mean the very broadest horizon of human understanding, along with the deepest well of personal experience. Of course, reason is far from perfect; we know we always run the risk of falling into rationalism. But we also realize that one of God's greatest gifts is that part of the human body that rests between our shoulders.

Thus, when it comes to defining faith and doctrine, unless we have all three legs grounded and balanced, the whole enterprise topples over. This means that whether we are talking about matters of religion, or milking a cow, keeping a modicum of stability is of great importance.

WHAT IS THE BOOK OF COMMON PRAYER?

In the Anglican tradition, the Book of Common Prayer is primarily a book of prayers and liturgical rites for public worship, though it also contains devotions for private or family use. It is called "common" because it contains the fixed texts of the regular services of the church used for public, or common, worship. It is also "common" because it uses the language of the people who are using it instead of a specialized "religious" language such as Latin or Hebrew. Lastly, it is "common" because it holds us together, something we share in common as we pray no matter what church we are attending or where we happen to be.

The Book of Common Prayer contains more than just prayers. There are also instructions for how to do the liturgies (called "rubrics"), biblical passages, and a lectionary that lists the Scripture readings for the year, statements of beliefs (creeds), and texts of songs (canticles). In addition to the well-known services of Holy Eucharist, it also includes services for Holy Baptism, Morning and Evening Prayer, weddings, ordinations, and funerals.

There are also a number of historical documents and a catechism—the basics of our faith in question-and-answer format. In many ways, the Book of Common Prayer defines and sets forth the faith and teaching of the Episcopal Church.

Lex orandi, lex credenda
Our praying shapes our believing
and our believing shapes our prayer.

HOW MANY HYMNALS ARE THERE?

Hymns draw all Episcopalians together musically in the same way that the Book of Common Prayer draws us together in prayer and liturgy. You may find several hymnals in the church pew!

The Hymnal 1982 offers 720 hymns in addition to liturgical music. While some of the hymns date back to monastic chants, this hymnal offers more modern music as well.

Lift Every Voice and Sing II is a popular collection of 280 musical pieces from both the African American and gospel traditions and has been compiled under the supervision of the Office of Black Ministries of the Episcopal Church. It includes service music and several psalm settings in addition to the Negro spirituals, gospel songs, and hymns.

Wonder, Love and Praise is an eclectic collection of two hundred hymns, songs, and spirituals including a large selection of service music and devotional pieces. It is a valuable resource for worship, church functions, and home use. There are additional hymns for Advent, Holy Week, Baptism, ordinations, and funerals as well as for healing, mission, unity, and peace.

My Heart Sings Out is a hymnal designed for all-age worship, with the aim of the full inclusion of children in weekly worship. Christian educators will find resources for all their needs, from church school to vacation programs.

POPULAR HYMNS FOR CHILDREN

Hymnody may be more important to children than it is to the octogenarians in your congregation. Hymns help incorporate children into the worshipping community. Hymns tell the story of our faith. Once learned, they will stick in their minds for when they become eighty years old.

The Hymnal 1982

#56	O come, O come, Emmanuel
#155	All glory, laud, and honor
#207	Jesus Christ is risen today, Alleluia!
#325	Let us break bread together on our knees
#405	All things bright and beautiful
#490	I want to walk as a child of the light
#554	'Tis the gift to be simple
#711	Seek ye first the kingdom of God

Wonder, Love, and Praise

#740	Wade in the water
#752	There's a sweet, sweet Spirit
#787	We are marching in the Light of God
#791	Peace before us
#797	It's me, it's me, it's me, O Lord
#812	I, the Lord of sea and sky

My Heart Sings Out (Church Publishing, 2005), compiled and edited by Fiona Vidal White, is a collection of music that captures the hearts of children that can also be used as a hymnal with children and families.

WHAT IS THE LECTIONARY?

A lectionary is a table of readings from Scripture appointed for reading at public worship. The association of particular texts with specific days began in the fourth century.

The Revised Common Lectionary (RCL) offers an option of semi-continuous reading of the great Old Testament narratives on the Sundays after Pentecost, to provide exciting new preaching opportunities, Vacation Bible School ideas, or informal summer storytelling for adults as well as children.

- ◆ **Year A:** Genesis through Judges
- ◆ **Year B:** the Davidic covenant and Wisdom literature
- ◆ **Year C:** the prophets—Elijah, Elisha, Amos, Hosea, Isaiah, Jeremiah, Joel, and Habbakuk

The Scriptures taken as a whole are foundational in God's revelation. Each part is to be heard in relation to every other part. Christianity is a religion of a person, Jesus Christ, and not a book. Because this is so, special authority is given to the Gospels, which contain the narrative of Jesus' life, death, resurrection, and of his teachings.

Each Sunday is provided with three lessons, or readings. One is from the Old Testament or Apocrypha. One is from the Epistles (letters), Acts of the Apostles, or the Revelation to John. One is from the Gospels. A psalm or canticle usually follows the Old Testament reading. The sequence hymn follows the second reading, or epistle.

DAYS AND SEASONS OF THE CHURCH YEAR

Advent

"Coming" in Latin, Advent is the first season of the Western Christian year. It has four Sundays; the first is the Sunday nearest November 30. The last day of Advent is always December 24, the day before Christmas. In Greek, Advent is translated from *parousia*, commonly used in reference to the Second Coming of the Messiah. Our lessons come from the prophets as we prepare for the coming of a King like no other. The color of this season is Sarum blue or purple.

Christmas

December 25 is the feast day on which we celebrate the birth of our Lord Jesus Christ. Our word "Christmas" comes from the old English *Christmasse* (Christ's Mass). In ancient calendars the feast was set close to the winter solstice, when the sun returned light to the world. Christmas is not just one day, but lasts for twelve— although the favorite song with "five golden rings" is a secular interpretation of what happens during that week of celebration. This season's color is white.

The Feast (and Season) of the Epiphany

This manifestation (revelation) of Christ to the Gentiles is observed on January 6. "Epiphany" comes from a Greek word meaning "showing forth, appearance, manifestation, revelation." The Feast of the Epiphany proclaims the good news that Jesus revealed God to all humanity. At Christmas the church celebrates the birth of Jesus, when God entered fully into the human experience. This Sunday takes the Christmas proclamation a step further, when the divine revelation in Jesus was revealed to the world as the magi came from the east. The eve of the Feast of the Epiphany (Twelfth Night) marks the end of the Christmas celebration. The Epiphany, January 6, is followed by a period of "Sundays after the Epiphany"; the length of the Epiphany season varies in length from four to nine Sundays, depending on the date of Easter that year. The Last Sunday of Epiphany is celebrated as Transfiguration Sunday. Green symbolizes our growth in understanding of Christ among us.

Lent

"Lent" comes from the Anglo-Saxon word *lencton*—the time of year when the days grow long. The season begins on Ash Wednesday and ends with the Easter Triduum that includes Maundy Thursday through Easter Sunday, covering forty days (excluding Sundays). Since every Sunday is a "little Easter" celebrating the Resurrection, Sundays remain feast days even during the solemn Lenten season. The five Lenten Sundays are followed by the Sunday of the Passion (Palm Sunday), which ushers in Holy Week. In the early church, Lent was the time of preparation for the Easter baptism of converts to the faith. Persons who were to receive the sacrament of baptism—"new birth," "death to sin"—were expected to fast and prepare during these weeks.

The Bible readings appointed for the five Sundays in Lent provide a short course in the meaning of baptism. The penitential color of purple designates this season.

Holy Week

The church dramatizes the events leading up to and including the suffering and death of Jesus on the cross. Holy Week begins with the Sunday of the Passion, or Palm Sunday, and the joyous triumphal entry into Jerusalem, and ends with the Triduum (*Triduum Sacrum*, meaning in Latin "the sacred three days"), which begins with the celebration of the Eucharist on Maundy Thursday and ends with the vespers of Easter Sunday evening. The name Maundy Thursday comes from the Latin *mandatum* or "command," from the words attributed to Jesus in the gospel of John: "I give you a new commandment, that you love one another. Just as I have loved you, you also should love one another" (John 13:34). Good Friday commemorates the crucifixion of our Lord. It is known as "Good" because of the new life brought about by his victory of the cross. Red (or black, if any color at all, on Good Friday) is used this week.

Easter

The principal feast day for Christians, this festival season of fifty days begins after sundown on Holy Saturday. The celebration of Easter is initiated with the Easter Vigil, which can be observed after sundown but ideally is kept just before sunrise, so that the proclamation of Jesus' resurrection comes with the dawn of the new day. The Easter season includes the events of Christ's resurrection and ascension and the coming of the Holy Spirit on the Day of Pentecost. The word "Easter" comes from *Eostre*, a Teutonic goddess whose name is associated with springtime, growth, and fertility. In most languages the name of the day is *Pascha*, which means "Passover." White is the color of joy—He is risen!

The Feast of the Ascension

Celebrated forty days after Easter Sunday (therefore always on a Thursday) it recalls our Lord's exaltation by being taken gloriously up into heaven. After Jesus' crucifixion and resurrection, Scripture tells us, he was seen for forty days before he ascended into heaven to be "seated at the right hand of God the Father." After Jesus' ascension, the disciples awaited the promised Spirit in Jerusalem. White reminds us of the joy of the Risen Christ.

Pentecost

From the Greek meaning "fiftieth day," this is the Christian feast that comes fifty days after Easter. It was the Greek name for the Hebrew Feast of Weeks, which fell on the fiftieth day after Passover that celebrated the calling of the Hebrews into a covenant relationship with God at Mt. Sinai. The time between Easter and Pentecost is known as the Great Fifty Days. The Feast of Pentecost celebrates the day that the Holy Spirit came to the disciples as they were gathered together in Jerusalem. The Book of Acts tells us that the Holy Spirit was like the rush of a mighty wind, with tongues of flame like fire that rested on each person. After Easter, Pentecost is the second most important feast of the church. The Feast of Pentecost has also been known as Whitsunday. This name probably came from the white robes worn on the day of baptism (White-Sunday). The flames of the Holy Spirit are red!

Trinity Sunday

The first Sunday after Pentecost, it has been part of the church year since 1334, when it was designated in commemoration of the doctrine of the Trinity, the belief that God is revealed to us in three persons existing in a mutual relationship of love. It is the total revelation of God: God the Father as Creator; God the Son as Redeemer; God the Holy Spirit as Sanctifier and Comforter. Our understanding of the Trinity arises from the biblical, creedal, and doctrinal statements that emerged from the creative struggles of theologians in the church to understand and talk about the nature of God. Again, white is used as a symbol of joy for the Triune God.

The Season after Pentecost

The numbered weeks after Pentecost are sometimes referred to as "Ordinary Time" because these weeks of the year are not associated with specific seasons, such as Lent and Easter, with their overriding themes. The Season after Pentecost begins with Trinity Sunday (the first Sunday after Pentecost) and ends on the last Sunday after Pentecost, just before Advent begins, sometimes called the Feast of Christ the King. The numbered Proper (appointed prayers and readings) to be used on each of the Sundays after Pentecost is determined by the calendar date of that Sunday (see BCP 158). The liturgical color for the Season after Pentecost is green, and these weeks during the summer and fall months in the northern hemisphere have often been connected with growth and fruitfulness in the Christian life. Although in this time of the church year it may seem that nothing of note happens, we understand that our "ordinary" lives is how we live out our Christian faith.

All Saints' Day

On November 1 the church remembers the saints of God—all faithful servants and believers. The day is seen as a communion of saints who have died and of all Christian persons. All Hallows' Eve, October 31 (from which our Hallowe'en traditions come); All Saints' Day, November 1; and All Souls' Day, November 2 (the Day of the Faithful Departed), are connected by tradition and are often celebrated together. The liturgical color for All Saints' Day is white, while specific saints' days are signified with the color red.

The Seasons of the Church Year

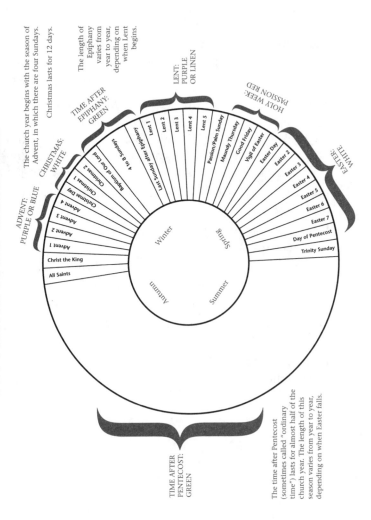

The church year begins with the season of Advent, in which there are four Sundays.

Christmas lasts for 12 days.

The length of Epiphany varies from year to year, depending on when Lent begins.

ADVENT: PURPLE OR BLUE

CHRISTMAS: WHITE

TIME AFTER EPIPHANY: GREEN

LENT: PURPLE OR LINEN

HOLY WEEK: PASSION RED

EASTER: WHITE

All Saints
Christ the King
Advent 1
Advent 2
Advent 3
Advent 4
Christmas Day
Christmas 1
Christmas 2
Baptism of Our Lord
4 to 8 Sundays
Last Sunday after Epiphany
Lent 1
Lent 2
Lent 3
Lent 4
Lent 5
Passion/Palm Sunday
Maundy Thursday
Good Friday
Vigil of Easter
Easter Day
Easter 2
Easter 3
Easter 4
Easter 5
Easter 6
Easter 7
Day of Pentecost
Trinity Sunday

Winter
Spring
Autumn
Summer

TIME AFTER PENTECOST: GREEN

The time after Pentecost (sometimes called "ordinary time") lasts for almost half of the church year. The length of this season varies from year to year, depending on when Easter falls.

HOW TO TEACH ABOUT SACRAMENTS

The two principal sacraments in the Episcopal Church are Baptism and Eucharist. Instituted by Jesus and celebrated over and over again in our congregations, they remind us who we are and to whom we belong. Hopefully all ages are present during worship to participate in these formational moments of our lives together.

- **Study** and compare the roots of these rites in your class. Jesus' baptism is found in all the gospels—Matthew 3:13–17, Mark 1:9–11, Luke 3:21–22, and John 1:29–34. The institution of the Lord's Supper is located in Matthew 26:26–29; Mark 14:22–25; Luke 22:14–23; and 1 Corinthians 11:23–26.
- **Practice** and act out various parts of each service. Find the order of service in the Book of Common Prayer.
- **Learn** the responses of the congregation for the services of Holy Eucharist and Holy Baptism.
- **Invite** the clergy to your class or ask the altar guild to bring the vessels that are used for everyone to see and touch.
- **Visit** the sacristy to see how the "table" is prepared.
- **Make** baptism cards for a baby or older person who is about to be baptized.
- **Process** as a class during the Offertory, bringing the bread and wine to the altar.

SPRINKLING, POURING, OR IMMERSION?

Holy Baptism is the sacrament by which God adopts us as his children and makes us members of Christ's Body, the church. In the Episcopal Church, baptism equals *full* membership in the church.

In the Episcopal Church, Holy Baptism takes place in the midst of the principle Sunday liturgy. In this way the whole faith community sees the action, hears the readings and the prayers, and perhaps most importantly, renews their own Baptismal Covenant. Baptisms are most commonly held on the four feast days of the church year: the Great Vigil of Easter, Pentecost, the Baptism of our Lord (in January), and All Saints' Day.

Baptism originally involved the total immersion of the body in water. The Greek term *baptize* means "to immerse." Baptism signifies the burial and death of sin and new life (resurrection) in Christ. Episcopal churches practice the pouring of water upon a candidate's head in most cases, but immersion is becoming more popular, reverting back to early church practices. Sprinkling offer

occurs when everyone present gets their share of water when the celebrant dips a pine branch in the font and liberally reminds everyone that we are all joined together in our baptisms.

Baptism requires water, much water, coming to the water, going down into the water, coming up out of the water. We need to get wet. By virtue of our baptism, we are all ministers of the church to represent Christ in the world according to the gifts given to us individually.

HOLY COMMUNION, MASS, OR EUCHARIST?

Depending on your church's liturgical style, you may find a variety of names for the Holy Eucharist in the Episcopal Church.

The Holy Eucharist is one of the two sacraments in the Episcopal Church. Christ commands it for the continual remembrance of his life, death, and resurrection, until his coming again.

It is also known as:

+ The Lord's Supper
+ Holy Communion
+ The Divine Liturgy
+ The Mass
+ The Great Offering

In the Episcopal Church all baptized members (including children) are welcome to receive the Eucharist in both forms—bread and wine. Children often prefer to intinct (dip) the bread (or wafer) into the chalice (cup) of wine during distribution.

While "first communion" classes and services are not part of the tradition of our church, it is advisable to offer Eucharist instruction classes for children *with* their parents to talk about this holy meal of thanksgiving. But they don't need to wait for a class in order to participate fully. All are welcome at God's Table!

WHAT *ARE* WE CONFIRMING?

The 1979 Book of Common Prayer describes baptism as "full initiation." Confirmation is a "pastoral rite" that publicly marks the mature affirmation of faith.

It is often a time when parents suddenly reappear at church, attending worship with their teenager in tow, coming to "complete" what they promised when they brought their infant to the church to be baptized. According to James Turrell, confirmation is not graduation and bears "neither a unique gift of the Spirit nor a meal ticket for communion."[2]

Confirmation is a public commitment to baptismal promises, made in the presence of a bishop, after which the person making the promises receives the bishop's blessing, signified by the imposition of hands. The candidates reaffirm their renunciation of evil and renew their commitment to Jesus Christ, and then they and

---

2. James F. Turrell, *Celebrating the Rites of Initiation* (New York: Church Publishing, 2013), 22.

the entire congregation join in the recitation of the baptismal covenant. No further promises are made.

Confirmation is not a rite of membership. That already took place at baptism, becoming part of the one holy catholic and apostolic church at that time. It does not make one an Episcopalian (or a Methodist or a Presbyterian). It is about the relationship between the candidate (who hopefully is making his or her own decision as opposed to mom or dad) and the Lord.

HOW TO MAKE A SECRET SIGNAL

Blessing oneself (aka "crossing oneself") is a ritual blessing made by members of many branches of Christianity. This blessing is made by the tracing of an upright cross or + across the body with the right hand, often accompanied by spoken or mental recitation of the Trinitarian formula—Father, Son, and Holy Spirit.

Children love to imitate adults, and you'll see them trying to copy a grown-up in the act of fluttering their hands across their forehead or chest. It may be helpful to practice some good old fashioned "show and tell" before they start creating their own secret symbols during worship. They can then create their own secret handshake for during the Peace.

The combination of the words and the action are a creed—a statement of belief. We mark ourselves as Christians through the sign of the cross, just as we are marked (invisibly) by the sign of the cross on our foreheads at baptism.

WHAT TO DO WHEN THE BISHOP SHOWS UP

Different from a visiting firefighter or interesting guest speaker, when the bishop comes to visit a congregation, get ready to clean your office. Don't make it too clean though—it will look like you don't really do anything. Organized clutter and combed hair is probably a good rule of thumb.

It can also be a time of anxiety for the clergy as well as vestry. Confirmation may also be part of the order of the day, with luncheons and, in some places, a chance for members of the church to get out their silver tea services. Yes, churches still do that.

Ask to be part of any planning meetings regarding the visitation. Consider yourself the advocate for children and youth so they can be active participants in any number of roles on that special day. Bishops love the photo op with someone that is from another generation.

Any number of rituals may take place on this day. One you may want to consider is the most complicated ritual in America today— the "wave" that often occurs at a football or baseball stadium. Your job may be to prep the youth group to strategically place themselves around the sanctuary to coordinate this symbolic act of joy.

If you're wondering what to call him or her, "Bishop" is appropriate. By the way, Episcopalians do *not* kiss the bishop's ring.

DO EPISCOPALIANS BELIEVE IN SAINTS?

Yes and no. In one of the prayers in the Book of Common Prayer we pray: "Almighty God, by your Holy Spirit you have made us one with your saints in heaven and on earth: Grant that in our earthly pilgrimage we may always be supported by this fellowship of love and prayer." This fellowship of love and prayer is the communion of saints affirmed in the Apostles' Creed.

Episcopalians do commemorate the feast days (usually the date of death) of Christians whose lives and deeds have been exemplary, whether or not they were of major ecclesiastical significance. We acknowledge that the Holy Spirit has been present in the lives of men and women across the ages, just as Christ continues to be present in our own day.

While we do not pray *to* these men and women, Episcopalians do get inspiration from their example and encouragement as we seek to be faithful in our own day.

Holy Women, Holy Men: Celebrating the Saints (Church Publishing, 2009) is a book that offers brief biographies of hundreds of these "saints" who are human just like us, sharing their stories as well as scripture passages that correspond to their lives' adventures.

"They lived not only in ages in past, there are hundreds and thousands still . . . and I mean to be one too!" *I Sing a Song of the Saints of God*, #293 in The Hymnal 1982

FIFTEEN FAMOUS EPISCOPAL CHRISTIAN EDUCATORS

1 **Anna Julia Cooper (1858–1964),** a distinguished scholar and educator, saw the status and agency of black women as central to the equality and progress of the United States. As active in church affairs as she was in the field of education, she delivered a particularly memorable address to a gathering of Episcopal clergy in Washington in 1886. In that speech she emphasized how the "quiet, chaste dignity and decorous solemnity" of Anglicanism attracted many "thinking colored men" and led them to seek membership in the Episcopal Church. She became the fourth African American woman to earn a doctoral degree, in 1924 at the age of sixty-five. Read: *A Voice from the South* (The Aldine Printing House, 1892).

2 **Adelaide Teague Case (1887–1948)** was interested in "progressive" religious education from the perspective of the Christian active in the world. Some of her areas of interest included the religious development of children, the teaching of religion for all ages, the Bible and religious education, social ethics, and peace education. Case became the first woman appointed to full professorial rank in any Episcopal or Anglican seminary, in 1941 when she joined the faculty of Episcopal Theological School in Cambridge, Massachusetts as professor of Christian education. Read: *Liberal Christianity and Religious Education* (Kessinger Publishing, 1924).

3 **Ruth Younger, CHS, (1897–1999)** was founder of a religious community (the Community of the Holy Spirit in 1952, which was the first Episcopal sisterhood that accepted women of color) and two schools (St. Hilda's and St. Hugh's, and the Melrose School in 1963), friend of hundreds of children and their parents, of bishops, priests, and laity across the continent, of businessmen and bankers. She was a pioneer in ecumenical relationships, a visionary with a strong practical bent, and an extraordinary woman with an extraordinary vocation.

4 **Dora P. Chaplin (1906–1990)** was educated in England, and taught at General Seminary from 1953 until retiring in 1971. In 1964 she was named a full professor, the first woman to become a full professor at the Episcopal seminary. Before that she was affiliated with the National Council of the Episcopal Church. Read: *The Privilege of Teaching* (Morehouse-Barlow, 1962) and *Children and Religion* (Charles Scribner's Sons, 1948).

5 **Randolph Crump Miller (1910–2002)** is considered one of the leading voices in Christian education in the twentieth century. Influencing the field for over sixty years, he published widely on the relationship between scripture, theology, and Christian education. He proposed that Christian education be centered in the Bible as "the primary source of our believing and our teaching as Christians." He served as a leader in both scholarly and denominational organizations and was the Horace Bushnell Professor Emeritus of Christian Nurture at Yale Divinity School for twenty-nine years. Read: *The Theory of Christian Education Practice: How Theology Affects Christian Education* (Religious Education Press, 1980).

6 **Kendig Brubaker Cully (1913–1987)** helped develop the M.A. degree program in religious education at Seabury-Western. This degree program was a response to the need of the Episcopal Church for directors of religious education at a time when the church had no one trained in the field. He taught at Seabury-Western for ten years (1953 to 1964) followed by a year as a professor of Christian education at New York Theological Seminary, where he was dean from 1965 to 1971. Read: *Harper's Encyclopedia of Religious Education* (Harper-Collins, 1990). He edited this volume along with his wife.

7 **Iris V. Cully (1914–2010)**, teacher-practitioner, writer theorist, and theologian of Christian education who, beginning in the late 1950s, helped promote a renewed emphasis on the role of Scripture at the center of Christian education. Iris was the first woman to earn a doctorate in religion from Northwestern University, the first woman on faculty at Yale Divinity School, the first professor at any Disciples of Christ school, and the first woman president of the Association of

Professors and Researchers in Religious Education. She believed the *kerygma*, or proclamation of the good news of God's action in Jesus Christ, forms the foundation of Christian education. Read: *The Bible in Christian Education* (Augsburg-Fortress, 2009).

8 **Verna J. Dozier (1917–2006),** a high school teacher of English literature and a religious educator, focused adult education on Bible study and on claiming the authority of the laity. She is credited by many in the Episcopal Church with actually changing the field of scripture study and reclaiming attention to the ministry of all the baptized. Read: *The Dream of God: A Call to Return* (Cowley, 1990) or *Confronted by God: The Essential Verna Dozier* (Seabury, 2006).

9 **Carman St. John Hunter (1922–2000)** was a mission educator at the Episcopal Church Center (1959–1963) and later (1963–1969) became the first woman head of a program unit (the Education for Mission and Ministry Unit) for the church-wide offices. She was a graduate of Western College for Women and a joint program of Columbia University and the Union and General Theological seminaries. A literacy expert, she translated Paulo Freire from the Portuguese and was a champion of adult literacy. Read: *Christian Education in the Episcopal Church: 1940s to 1970s* (Episcopal Church Center, 1987).

10 **Charles Winters (1924–)** was professor of systematic theology at the University of the South, Sewanee, Tennessee (1954–1980). In 1975, together with his wife and colleague, **Lillian "Flower" Ross (1929–2009)** he developed the *Education for Ministry* (EfM) program to prepare primarily Episcopal laypersons to fulfill their baptismal ministry in the world. Their praxis-oriented vision of Christian education continues to inform educational endeavors at the congregational, seminary, and university levels.

11 **Locke E. Bowman, Jr., (1930–),** an experienced teacher and author, his books were often practical "how to" instructional guides on effective teaching techniques and resources for teachers in Christian education. He was one of the first to set specific standards and objectives for improving teaching in

the church and provided a wealth of resources for all phases of church education. Dr. Bowman was a professor of Christian education and pastoral theology (1983–1994) at Virginia Theological Seminary where he was also the founder for the Center for the Ministry of Teaching and visionary for the *Episcopal Children's Curriculum*. Read: *Straight Talk About Teaching in Today's Church* (Westminster John Knox Press, 1967).

⑫ Joseph P. Russell (1932–2004) was known for his special gift of using storytelling to shape a sense of identity, and the power of worship to form Christians in every generation. He served in the Diocese of Oregon and was Canon of Education and Program in the Diocese of Ohio. He danced with the Book of Common Prayer in one hand and the Bible in the other. Read: *Sharing Our Biblical Story: A Guide to Using Liturgical Reading as the Core of Church and Family Education* (Morehouse, 1988).

⑬ John H. Westerhoff, III (1933–), an Episcopalian priest and professor at Duke University Divinity School for twenty years, advocated through his writing, teaching, pastoring, and editorial work an enculturation model he called "catechesis" or Christian formation. His dominant concern has been to help the church move from a schooling model of Christian education to a catechetical model of Christian formation. Read: *Will Our Children Have Faith?, 3rd edition* (Morehouse, 2012).

⑭ Fredrica Harris Thompsett (1942–) is the Mary Wolfe Professor Emerita of Historical Theology at the Episcopal Divinity School in Cambridge, Massachusetts, where she also served as the first woman (and lay) academic dean for fourteen years. A teacher, prolific author, and scholar of Anglican theology and history, her passion is the ministry of all the baptized—laity and clergy. A champion of lifelong Christian formation and Christian educators, she reminds us that everyone is a theologian, fed by the waters of our baptism. Read: *We Are Theologians* (Seabury, 2003).

⑮ Jerome Berryman (1937–) is the founder of Godly Play and Senior Fellow of the Center for the Theology of Childhood. He has authored numerous books, including *Children and the Theologians* (Morehouse, 2009).

YOUR SANITY

STRESS? WHAT STRESS?

Does your back ache, your head pound, are your shoulders knotted? Does your stomach hurt, is your digestion out of whack? How's your blood pressure, your cholesterol, your heart rate? Do you catch every little "bug" that seems to go around?

You may be overstressed. Yes, that does happen to Christian educators. Being called by God to this ministry is not immunization from the malady called "burn out."

The prescription:

- Eat-sleep-play-work right. Count the calories, count the hours, and take your day off.
- Stay in touch with God: pray, meditate, listen, dance, discern, share, journal, garden, do yoga—whatever feeds you spiritually.
- Join Forma (*www.episcoforma.org*).
- Join (or form) a colleagues' group with others in your area and meet for lunch or coffee once a month.
- Develop a plan for your continuing education and annual silent retreat.
- Find a spiritual director.
- Close the door to your office for at least fifteen minutes per day and put a sign on the door "Do Not Disturb: Praying."
- Listen to music. Light a candle. Burn some incense.
- Say "no" next time.

HOW TO TAKE CARE
OF YOURSELF

I hereby command you: Be strong and courageous; do not be frightened or dismayed, for the Lord your God is with you wherever you go. (Joshua 1:9)

- Clarify your job responsibilities, both what you will and won't be expected to do.
- Make certain the church understands what it has promised to offer in terms of support and finances.
- Find someone who will back you up as "second in command," helping when the workload is heavy, stepping in if you are sick or out of town.
- Find a trusted confidant who will agree to let you vent frustrations and brainstorm solutions to problems as they come along.
- Delegate.
- Solicit feedback from volunteers on a regular basis.
- Add your own ideas that work for you:

Those who wait for the Lord shall renew their strength, they shall mount up with wings like eagles, they shall run and not be weary, they shall walk and not faint. (Isaiah 40:31)

TIME BANDITS

Most churches don't have time clocks with which to punch in and out, and the 9 to 5 rule rarely applies for those who work in the church.

Hints to keep your time in check so that it doesn't suck the life out of you:

- Plan each day.
- Prioritize your tasks.
- Say no to nonessential tasks.
- Delegate.
- Take the time you need to do a quality job (so you won't have to do it over again due to errors).
- Break large, time-consuming tasks into smaller tasks.
- Practice the ten-minute rule. Work on a dreaded task for ten minutes each day.
- Evaluate how you're spending your time. Keep a log of when you work, even it if is at home.
- Limit distractions. Okay, this may not work when the ladies' auxiliary meets, as they will constantly stop by your office to chat.
- Don't look at your work e-mail on your day off.
- Take your day off.
- Take your day off.
- Take your day off.

TWO HEADS ARE BETTER THAN ONE

You may think you can do it all yourself. Others may assume you can do it all yourself. *Not!* If your church does not have a committee to help you steer your program area, put one together ASAP.

A small group that is responsible for guiding the overall formation for the congregation helps you articulate a vision for the educational and formational ministries, develops an overall plan for teaching and learning, and helps you pay attention to the way its work impacts and supports the work of other ministry groups. Goal setting and evaluation on an annual basis should be a priority.

This is the group that can be your cheerleader as well as your council of advice. They can make sure your job description is accurate to the expectations (and reality) under which you are living out your position. Most of all, they can pray for you!

Some tips for forming an education committee:

- **Membership:** a church school teacher or two, a parent or two, a vestry person, an outreach committee member, a worship committee member. All of these areas impact Christian formation.
- **Meet:** monthly or quarterly (with refreshment).
- **Method:** Send out an agenda in advance. Keep communication open throughout the year. Begin gatherings in prayer.

HOW *NOT* TO WORK FOR FREE

Many Christian educators are volunteers who put in countless hours in their congregation to ensure children and youth have a voice and program to go to. However, there does come a time that leadership in the church needs to know what you are doing and the amount of time you are spending to accomplish it.

If you are a part-time employee, keep track of your hours. If you get paid for twenty hours a week, and work forty, make sure you are logging your hours and the projects and tasks you are doing during this time. When it comes time for a job review, evaluation of your salary, or determination to keep or cut your position, you will have a record to show exactly what is involved to plan and implement a solid educational ministries program.

You may even want to consider working only the amount of time you are paid for. After all, whatever extra you are doing is like working for free. Aren't you worth it?

How many times have you heard of a church removing the Christian Educator or youth minister position from a parish budget, thinking volunteers could cover the slack? Then, surprise! They discover that there was much more to this "little job" than anyone anticipated.

Advocate for yourself—and track what you do! You are worth it!

HOW TO BE THE REAL BOSS: PRAY

When we are at high altitudes we are told to drink lots of water. When the oxygen mask pops down on a flight, we are told to fix our mask before helping others. As we mentor and build faith in others, we can't forget our own spiritual well-being.

Most of us need to discipline ourselves in order to include a specific time for prayer each day. When we do take time to talk with God our day seems to run smoother.

- **Worship in different places and traditions.** Find a place to worship where you are not in charge and attend services at least quarterly.
- **Go outside.** Find a tree and lean against it, and recognize the God-given strength that comes from the earth.
- **Find a spiritual mentor.** Meet with him or her regularly to discuss your spiritual life and practices that encourage growth.
- **Read Scripture devotionally.** Meditating on one verse a day is better than none.
- **Try a new practice or discipline.** Contemplative prayer, silence, prayer groups, *Lectio Divina*, walking a labyrinth, and writing prayers are just a few examples.

HOW TO LOCATE TOILET PAPER

Christian educators are known for having the pulse on a variety of events, topics, and supplies in the church. That includes when a restroom runs out of paper towels, the tablecloth for coffee hour is missing, or the copier has a paper jam.

Get a lay of the land of your church and become best friends with the sexton (janitor). Hopefully he or she also works on Sunday mornings, because that's when things seem to break. Bring him or her coffee every now and then, along with a donut. Bribery does work. Develop a way to text him or her when something is amiss so that he or she can rescue you.

Just in case, get a key to the closet where these supplies are held for emergency purposes. But don't tell anyone you have it. You may also want to use it as a hiding place.

You still may get a tap on the shoulder when you are kneeling, deep in prayer, in the midst of a service, or when you are changing a diaper. The ladies' room may be out of toilet paper.

HOW TO UNTANGLE
THE TRIANGLE

Surprise—working in the church is not always loving, caring, sugar and spice and everything nice. As humans, we are tempted to seek our own will instead of the will of God. So we screw up. All of us. And that leads to conflict.

The first conflict faced by humanity was the triangulation of Adam and Eve (regarding a snake and God). Pilate and the crowd deciding Jesus' fate is another.

Some steps for resolving conflict:

+ Practice self management—step back, get perspective.
+ Diagram the triangles—who is involved, what patterns do you observe, are you in the middle?
+ Play the appropriate role for your position in church relationships—as a staff person, you are in a position of power; use it wisely.
+ Be as neutral as possible.

Ask yourself:

+ What buttons do you have? How can you avoid them being pushed?
+ What crisis has the church faced in the past? How did it come though?
+ Who are the most thoughtful people in leadership in the congregation? How can you connect with them?

E-MAIL COMPLAINTS

Be careful how you communicate with children and families about faith practices at home—especially if they involve changes around the holidays. They can lead to some disturbing e-mails.

Dear teacher,

Following your suggestions, I made a list of things that are life-giving to our family for this Christmas season and cut everything else. We added a new tradition of nightly lighting a lantern to let Mary and Joseph know that we "have room at our inn." Our son Billy is a nervous wreck that he's going to have to share his bunk bed with them.

Thanks a lot,
A perplexed mother

(*An actual note received by Kim McPherson at St. John's Cathedral in Denver, Colorado.*)

SPIRITUAL DIRECTION

Also known as spiritual companions or spiritual guides, spiritual directors help people discover how God is truly with them every day and everywhere.

You might seek spiritual direction for a variety of reasons, including to:

* Identify and trust your own experiences of God.
* Integrate spirituality into your daily life.
* Discern and make difficult choices.
* Share your hopes, struggles, and losses.
* Develop a sensitivity for justice and concern for the poor.
* Live the essence of your spiritual affiliation with integrity.

Spiritual direction is not really about being *directed*. Rather, it is very much about being encouraged to draw closer to God. As someone who is probably working and not worshipping much on a Sunday morning, you'll need space and time to connect with God. Spiritual direction can help you reclaim that piece of your spiritual life that often gets put at the bottom of your "to-do list," even after picking up the graham crackers for next Sunday's kindergarten snack.

> *Do not worry about anything, but in everything by prayer and supplication with thanksgiving let your requests be made known to God.* (Philippians 4:6)

HOW TO FORGIVE SOMEONE

Forgiving is one of the most difficult disciplines of faith, since it seems to cost you something additional when you've already been wronged. Swallowing your pride and seeking a greater good, however, can yield great healing and growth.

- **Acknowledge that God forgives you.** When you realize that God has already shown you forgiveness, and continues to forgive sinners like you, it's easier to forgive someone else.

- **Consult Scripture.** Jesus taught the Lord's Prayer to his disciples, who were hungry to become like he was. Forgiveness is a big part of this. Read Matthew 6:9–15.

- **Seek the person out whenever possible.** Consciously decide to deliver your forgiveness in person. *Note*: This may not be wise in all cases, given the timing of the situation or the level of hurt. Consult with a good friend before taken questionable action.

- **Say, "I forgive you," out loud.** A verbal declaration of forgiveness is ideal. Speaking the words enacts a physical chain reaction that can create healing for both speaker and hearer. In the Bible, Jesus used these words to heal a paralyzed man from across a room.

- **Pray for the power to forgive.** Praying for this is always good, whether a forgiveness situation is at hand or not. It is especially helpful in cases where declaring forgiveness may be beyond your reach.

HOW TO CHOOSE THE RIGHT VIRGIN MARY

Around the first week of Advent families come out of the woodwork. It must mean that rehearsals for the annual Christmas pageant have begun. And every little girl (and her mother) thinks she would make the *best* Mary.

Qualifications for the role of Mary:

- must look good in a blue head scarf
- can sit still on a little bench (or the floor) for an extended period of time
- is not allergic to hay, straw, or angel glitter
- gets along with whoever is cast as Joseph
- has the capability to ponder things in her heart
- has parents who will not show up with a film crew on opening night
- is not your own child, due to the appearance of favoritism

Best advice—find a team of parents to oversee the annual Christmas pageant production. Let them worry about it.

HOW TO CONSOLE OTHERS

Consolation is a gift from God. Christians in turn give it to others to build up the body of Christ and preserve it in times of trouble (see Corinthians 1:4–7). Episcopalians also employ food as a helpful secondary means.

- **Listen first.** Make it known that you're present and available. When the person opens up, be quiet and attentive.
- **Be ready to help the person face grief with sadness.** The object is to help the person name, understand, and work through his or her feelings, not gloss over them.
- **Avoid saying things to make yourself feel better.** "I know exactly how you feel," is seldom true and trivializes the sufferer's pain. Even if you have experienced something similar, no experience is exactly the same. If there is nothing to say, simply be present with the person.
- **Show respect with honesty.** Don't try to answer the mysteries of the universe or force your beliefs on the person. Be clear about the limitations of your abilities. Be ready to let some questions go unanswered. Consolation isn't about having all the answers; it's about bearing one another's burdens.
- **Don't put words in God's mouth.** Avoid saying, "This is God's will," or, "This is part of God's plan." Unless you heard it straight from God, don't say it.

HOW TO COPE WITH GRIEF AND LOSS

Episcopalians tend to downplay their losses by saying, "Oh, I'm fine, thanks." This may provide only temporary relief at best. Any loss can cause pain, feelings of confusion, and uncertainty. These responses are normal. And in your role as a Christian educator, you will be faced with opportunities you don't anticipate that will impact your ministry.

- **Familiarize yourself with the stages of grief.** Experts identify five: denial, anger, bargaining, depression, and acceptance. Some add hope as a sixth stage. Grieving persons cycle back and forth through the stages, sometimes experiencing two or three in a single day. This is normal.

- **Express your grief.** Healthy ways may include crying, staring into space for extended periods, ruminating, shouting at the ceiling, and sudden napping. Laughing outbursts are also appropriate and should not be judged too harshly.

- **Identify someone you trust to talk to.** Available people can include a spouse, parents, relatives, friends, a doctor, your spiritual director, or a trained counselor. Many household pets also make good listeners and willing confidants.

- **Choose a personal way to memorialize the loss.** Make a collage of photographs, offer a memorial donation in the loved one's name to an organization that supports his or her passion, or start a scrapbook of memories to honor the event. This helps you begin to heal without getting stuck in your grief.

HOW TO BLESS A CHILD (OR ANYONE ELSE)

Blessings through history have had many purposes, often involving the passing of wealth or property from one person or generation to another. A Christian blessing is a declaration of the gospel of Jesus Christ to a specific individual—an affirmation that another person is claimed and loved by almighty God. Blessings should be dispensed liberally and with abandon.

* **Evaluate the need at hand.**

    People have different needs at different times. When you perceive a need in which a blessing appears appropriate, take time to discern.

* **Use safe touch.**

    Human touch is an affirmation with profound physical effects. Healing and emotional release are common. Make sure you use touch that is non-threatening, respectful, and communicates the love of Christ.

* **Choose an appropriate way to give the blessing.**

    ◇ Position one or both hands on the person's head.

    ◇ Use a light touch, but one firm enough to let the person know that he or she is being blessed.

    ◇ Place one hand on the person's shoulder.

    ◇ Trace a cross on the person's forehead.

    ◇ Hold both of the person's hands in yours while making good eye contact.

* **Make a declaration of freedom.**

    ◇ Blessings are often most effective when the spoken word is employed. For example: "[insert name here], child of God, you have been sealed by the Holy Spirit and marked with the cross of Christ forever."

    ◇ Consider ad-libbing a verbal blessing that speaks directly to the situation.

- ✧ Whenever possible, include the words spoken at baptism: "In the name of the Father, and of the Son, and of the Holy Spirit."

- **Be aware.**

  Indirect blessings are often appropriate. These include but are not limited to favors, prayers, kind words, consolation, a hot meal, shared laughter, and acceptance. Some cultures consider head touching impolite or even rude, so always ask permission before making a blessing this way.

HOW TO DRAW THE LINE

Setting boundaries is one of the most important parts of relationships and ministry. Without agreeable boundaries, most relationships cannot function well. The expression "Good fences make good neighbors" is true.

- Know yourself—your needs and your limits. What are your values, priorities, and non-negotiables? Get a handle on them.
- Don't fall victim to the "disease to please."
- Identify the boundary situations that are most difficult for you. Do they involve bossy people, passive people, or those who have different values?
- Identify strategies that have worked in the past to implement when needed.
- What do you need to do (if anything) to regain your personal power or stand up for yourself? Be firm, gracious, and direct.
- Develop good relationships, even with those with whom you may not want to. It will pay off in the long run.
- Charm works wonders. As does chocolate.
- Sometimes you'll just have to throw in the towel.

HOW TO AVOID EASTER EGG CATASTROPHES

Early Sunday morning, my mom helped me hide about 350 Easter eggs in the churchyard, as we've done every year since I took this position and my predecessor did before me. This year, just as we finished, a squirrel scampered down the big oak tree, sat down with a bright purple plastic egg, and worked patiently with his little fingers at the crack in the middle. I walked over, gently shooing him away. I assume Easter candy is no better for squirrels than it is for dogs. That little bugger managed to cram the whole egg in his mouth and scrambled back up from whence he'd come, only dropping the egg when he had reached a height guaranteed to break it all apart upon impact.

As I laughed with my mom and some of the youth group who'd happened along, another squirrel infiltrated, leaving an open egg and a Milky Way wrapper behind.

Before we knew it we were under attack, with several squirrels and a blue jay coming after our eggs, which we'd planned to leave outside until after the service when the hunt takes place, of course! I hired four young men for "squirrel patrol," and with their parents' blessings they stayed outdoors during the service, shooing off all bestial attacks on our eggs with nothing but a lacrosse stick and a foam mini soccer ball. The soccer ball, purple egg, and Milky Way were the only known victims of the assault.

—CHRISTINA CLARK, FAMILY MINISTER AT ST. BARNABAS, DENVER

BIBLE STUFF

WHO WROTE THE BIBLE?

The short answer is: God. The long answer is . . . much longer.

As we all know, the Bible is not a book, but a collection of books—sixty-six (plus the Apocrypha) put together by dozens of authors. These books span more than a thousand years and include many different genres, like history, poetry, praise, wisdom, and prophecy. It's no surprise that each book has its own story of authorship, and thanks to the black hole of antiquity we simply don't have answers to a lot of important questions.

While many Christians have a more traditional view—that the Bible was divinely and inerrantly written by the hand of God—Episcopalians tend to see it a bit differently. Many of us view the Bible as the word of God that comes to us through humans. Thus the biases, preferences, and prejudices these authors carried may be, to some degree, present in the final product. There is almost universally agreed-upon evidence of addition and subtraction that has occurred in the compiling of our most sacred book. This does not make the Bible any less "true" but it does help us better understand it.

We do know that two communities, ancient Israel and the emerging Christian community, primarily wrote the Bible. The latest scholarship suggests that some books, like the Gospels (Matthew, Mark, Luke, and John), were indeed the products not so much of these individuals, but of the communities to which they were tied.

There is no doubt that these holy men and women, moved by God, participated in bringing these great writings to us. So we tend to see the Bible's origins less as a divine product with divine authority and more as a human response to the presence and action of God.

What's more, we believe God is still writing. While we're not about to suggest any additions to the Bible, we are alert to ways the Living God continues to inform us and communicate with us. Our quest for authorship is ongoing, as is our search for the ways God continues to speak and actively move in our lives.

One Episcopal thinker likes to describe the way many of us see the Bible as historical, metaphorical, and sacramental. Historical, meaning it is a product of its time, not written to us or for us, but nonetheless incredibly illuminating. Metaphorical, in that it is more than literal, and more than factual, and we are less concerned with how it happened than what it means. And sacramental, referring to the Bible's ability to mediate the sacred; in other words, how is this book working as a vehicle of the Holy Spirit in our lives?

Episcopalians don't tend to take the Bible literally, but we do take it seriously. This includes paying attention to the latest archaeological findings that help us understand the history and origins of the Scriptures.

A GUIDE TO POPULAR BIBLE TRANSLATIONS

Translation (Abbreviation)	Date	Reading Level	Translation Method	Translators
Common English Bible (CEB)	2010 (NT) 2011 (OT)	7th grade	Hybrid: Verbal equivalence with dynamic balance and common language	CEB Committee, an alliance of five denominational publishers (120 translators, 24 faith traditions, 500 readers from 13 denominations)
Contemporary English Version (ESV)	1995	5th grade	Dynamic equivalence	American Bible Society
English Standard Version (ESV)	2001; rev. 2007	11th grade	Verbal equivalence	Crossway (100 evangelical scholars, primarily from the Reformed tradition)
Good News Bible/ Today's English Version (TEV)	1976	6th grade	Dynamic equivalence	American Bible Society
King James Version (KJV)	1611, 1769	12th grade	Verbal equivalence	54 English scholars
The Living Bible (LB)	1971	8th grade	Paraphrase of American Standard Bible	Kenneth Taylor
The Message	1933 (NT), 2001 (OT)	6th grade	Paraphrase from original languages	Eugene Peterson
New American Bible (NAB)	1970; NT rev. 1986	7th grade	Dynamic equivalence, 1970; verbal equivalence, 1986	Confraternity of Christian Doctrine (Roman Catholic)
New International Version (NIV)	1978; rev. 2010	8th grade	Hybrid: verbal equivalence with dynamic balance	Biblica. (Original NIV translated by 110 multi-denomination scholars; 2010 update by 10-person Committee on Bible translators)

Continued

Translation (Abbreviation)	Date	Reading Level	Translation Method	Translators
New Internationals Reader's Version (NIrV)	1996	3rd grade	Verbal equivalence with dynamic balance and some simplification	Biblica (40, including stylists)
New Jerusalem Bible	1985	8th grade	Verbal equivalence, with dynamic tendencies	Approximately 30
New Living Translation (NLT)	1996 rev. 2007	6th grade	Dynamic equivalence	Tyndale House Foundation (90 scholars from a variety of theological and denominational backgrounds)
New Revised Standard Version (NRSV)	1990	11th grade	Verbal equivalence	National Council of Churches (30 scholars)
The Voice	2008 (NT)	8th grade	Paraphrase	Thomas Nelson Publishers and Ecclesia Bible Society (27 scholars and 52 re-tellers from the emergent movement)

Definitions:

Dynamic equivalence: Emphasis is on reproducing the functional meaning of the ancient words with freedom to rearrange the order of the words (syntax) in the target language.

Verbal equivalence: Emphasis is on reproducing the modern English equivalent of the ancient words, with tendency to use same word order as the ancient language.

Paraphrase: Emphasis is on expressing the meaning in contemporary language, with numerous additional words.

HOW TO CHOOSE A BIBLE

There is a dizzying variety of Bible storybooks and regular Bibles to choose from. They all come with illustrations, study notes, and other special features. But which one is the best? Here are some general tips to help you make your choice:

Each child should have his or her own Bible. Owning a Bible shows how important God's Word is and how it should always be on hand as the practical guidebook for life. Look for children and teen Bibles that contain the whole text of the Bible as well as additional materials to help understand and apply what is read.

Preschool: Buy a Bible storybook, with simple illustrations, that covers key Bible stories and has a small number of simple words per picture.

Beginning Readers: Choose a storybook that contains simple illustrations and more stories than a preschool storybook. It is best if beginning readers have a storybook that takes two pages or more to tell each story.

Elementary Age: Fewer pictures and more words is the key at this level. Make sure the illustrations are interesting and up-to-date. Simple Bible reference lists and an index are also good features to look for at this age level.

Teens: Choose a Bible with all or some of the following features: a simple concordance, explanatory notes in the text, introductions to each book of the Bible, maps of Bible lands, cross-references, and Bible facts or trivia. Be careful not to belittle scripture to a language so common and accessible that it completely misses the original intention of what was written (under God's revelation) by the authors. If a paraphrase is used, make sure a solid translation is nearby when doing Bible study for comparison.

Adults: Same as teens. Some good examples: Cambridge Annotated Study Bible (Cambridge) NRSV, HarperCollins Study Bible (Harper-Collins) NRSV, New Oxford Annotated Bible (Oxford) NRSV, Oxford Study Bible (Oxford) REB, The Access Bible (Oxford) NRSV.

HOW TO PRESENT A BIBLE

The presentation of Bibles to children is a tradition in many churches. There seem to be three different times during the year when this is most prevalent: in September when the academic year begins, on the First Sunday of Advent, and at the end of the academic year in May or June. Many churches give children Bibles in third or fourth grade, since that is the age when they are learning the skills to be able to read chapter books.

Develop a practice of presenting children a Bible (a version that can remain with them as they grow older) at the beginning of the academic year. They can be encouraged to bring it with them to class where they can learn how to use it and where to find the stories they are studying. Help your teachers incorporate Bible study skills in the context of your regular curriculum. Encourage parents to keep the Bible available (and not put it on a shelf), read from it during family time, before bedtime, or on occasions of quiet time.

When Bibles are presented, do it the context of your worship service. Recognize the importance of passing along the stories of our faith from one generation to another. Glue bookplates on the inside cover, noting your church's name, location, and the date.

Presentation and Blessing of Bibles

Presider: Receive the gift of this Bible so that the story of God and God's people may be with you at home, church, or wherever you shall choose to carry it. Enjoy reading how God is at work in nature and history. Learn about the life and teachings of Jesus. Be open to how God may continue to speak to you through your reading of the scriptures.

Please hold out your Bibles extended in front of you and let us pray:

(*Extending hands in prayer*)

Blessed be your name, O Lord our God, You are the fount and source of every blessing! You have revealed yourself to your human creation in many and diverse ways. Our memory of your revelation is maintained and reverenced in the Scriptures that we hold in our hands. Look with delight upon us today as we renew our commitment to read and remember you in the stories of our salvation. Help us to absorb its wisdom and live its inspired truth.

Encourage us with the help of the Holy Spirit to use these sacred writings for our prayer and inspiration, for the increase of our own faith and devotion, and for the building up of your Kingdom. Through your Word may we be transformed into the very likeness of Christ, your Son, who lives and reigns with you forever and ever. Amen.

HOW EPISCOPALIANS READ THE BIBLE (AND WHY MORE SHOULD)

It's the best selling book of all time—and possibly the least read.

Polls come out annually showing how many Bibles people own (the average American home has four), yet how utterly clueless we are about what's in it. A recent poll says 10 percent of us believe Joan of Arc was Noah's wife. While Episcopalians probably score about average in this category, it's not for lack of exposure, or a definite interpretive model toward understanding the Holy Scriptures.

In general, Episcopalians have two rules when it comes to interpreting the Bible. The first is that we read it together. The second is that we interpret it responsibly. As children of the English Reformation, which brought us the English Bible (you can thank us later), we are strong believers in everyone's ability to read and interpret Scripture. We like to think that the observations of the farmhand, the homemaker, the nurse, and the auto mechanic are integral to arriving at what it is the Scriptures are saying to us.

However, we also believe there is a place for reasoned, informed, and educated opinion on the matter. When we read the Bible we are apt to do so alongside a study book called a commentary. We also think it fitting to hold and attend classes that expose us to the finest Bible scholarship available. And Episcopalians believe in and rely on an educated clergy who go through a minimum three-year graduate divinity program. Parishioners often look to clergy as resources for Bible interpretation.

Despite these convictions, Episcopalians are usually the first ones to admit we're not Bible experts. Many of us think we should read the Bible more often. And many of us are thankful that we have much knowledge at hand should we decide to do so. Although we still wouldn't know who Noah's wife was; the Bible never names her.

BUT NO ONE SHOWS UP FOR BIBLE STUDY!

Every survey you'll take asking for topics that adults want to happen in your church will result in Bible study as #1. So, you'll add that to the offerings and put it on the calendar, but no one shows up. What's up with that?

Some possible answers:

- Bible study is good for everyone except those who answer surveys.
- Only the rector should lead a Bible study (after all, they know all the answers) but the rector is a lousy teacher.
- Adults really want to learn how to make sense of what they hear on Sunday in their daily life only during the sermon.
- The coffee served tastes like mud.
- They're too embarrassed to admit they don't own a Bible.
- They learn all they need to know about the Bible on Jeopardy!
- Wednesday at 11:00 a.m. isn't convenient since they work two jobs.
- There's enough violence on the evening news.
- Waiting for it to come out on Netflix.
- No chocolate for snacks.

THE SEVEN FUNNIEST BIBLE STORIES

Humor isn't scarce in the Bible; you just have to look for it. For example, God tells Abraham (100 years old) and Sarah (in her 90s) they'll soon have a son. Understandably, they laugh. Later, they have a son named Isaac, which means "he laughs." Bible humor is also ironic, gross, and sometimes just plain bizarre.

1 Gideon's dog-men (Judges 6:11–7:23):

God chooses Gideon to lead an army against the Midianites. Gideon gathers an army of 32,000 men, but this is too many. God tells Gideon to make all the men drink from a stream, and then selects only the 300 men who lap water like dogs.

2 David ambushes Saul in a cave while he's "busy" (1 Samuel 24:2–7):

While pursuing David cross-country to engage him in battle, Saul goes into a cave to "relieve himself" (move his bowels). Unbeknownst to Saul, David and his men are already hiding in the very same cave. While Saul's doing his business, David sneaks up and cuts off a corner of Saul's cloak with a knife. Outside afterward, David shows King Saul the piece of cloth to prove he could have killed him "on the throne."

3 King David does the goofy (2 Samuel 12–23):

David is so excited about bringing the Ark of the Covenant to Jerusalem that he dances before God and all the people dressed only in a linen ephod, an apron-like garment that covered only the front of his body.

4 Lot's wife (Genesis 19:24–26):

While fleeing God's wrath upon the cities of Sodom and Gomorrah, Lot's wife forgets (or ignores) God's warning not to look back upon the destruction and turns into a woman-sized pillar of salt.

The doomed city of Sodom

Pillar of salt (formerly Lot's wife)

Lot's wife ignored God's warning. She looked back at the city of Sodom and became a pillar of salt.

5 Gerasene demoniac (Mark 5:1–20):

A man is possessed by so many demons that chains cannot hold him. Jesus exorcises the demons and sends them into a herd of 2,000 pigs, which then run over the edge of a cliff and drown in the sea. The herders, now 2,000 pigs poorer, get miffed and ask Jesus to leave.

6 Disciples and loaves of bread (Mark 8:14–21):

The disciples were there when Jesus fed 5,000 people with just five loaves of bread and two fish. They also saw him feed 4,000 people with seven loaves. Later, in a boat, the disciples fret to an exasperated Jesus because they have only one loaf for 13 people.

7 Peter can't swim (Matthew 14:22–33):

Blundering Peter sees Jesus walking on the water and wants to join him. But when the wind picks up, Peter panics and starts to sink. In Greek, the name Peter means "rock."

Peter, "the rock," sank when he looked to himself instead of to Jesus. Jesus later described Peter as a Rock of the church (Matthew 16:18).

THE TOP 10 BIBLE MIRACLES (AND WHAT THEY MEAN)

1 Creation.

God created the universe and everything that is in it, and God continues to create and recreate without ceasing. God's first and ongoing miracle was to reveal that the creation has a purpose.

2 The Passover.

Pharaoh enslaved the Israelites, believing the people belonged to him, not to God. In the last of 10 plagues, God visited the houses of all the Egyptians to kill the firstborn male in each one. God alone is Lord of the people, and no human can claim ultimate power over us.

3 The Exodus.

God's people were fleeing Egypt when Pharaoh dispatched his army to force them back into slavery. The army trapped the people with their backs to a sea, but God parted the water and the people walked across to freedom while Pharaoh's minions were destroyed. God chose to free us from all forms of tyranny so we may use that freedom to serve God and each other.

4 Manna.

After the people crossed the sea to freedom, they complained that they were going to starve to death. They even asked to go back to Egypt. God sent manna, a form of bread, so the people lived. God cares for us even when we give up, pine for our slavery, and lose faith. God never abandons us.

5 The Incarnation.

The immortal and infinite God became a human being, choosing to be born of a woman. God loved us enough to become one of us in Jesus of Nazareth, forever bridging the divide that had separated us from God.

6 Jesus healed the paralyzed man.

Some men brought a paralyzed friend to Jesus. Jesus said, "Son, your sins are forgiven" (Mark 2:5). This means that Jesus has the power to forgive our sins—and he does so as a free gift.

7 Jesus calmed the storm.

Jesus was asleep in a boat with his disciples when a great storm came up and threatened to sink it. He said, "Peace! Be still!" (Mark 4:39). Then the storm immediately calmed. Jesus is Lord over even the powers of nature.

8 The Resurrection.

Human beings executed Jesus, but God raised him from the dead on the third day. Through baptism, we share in Jesus' death, so we will also share in eternal life with God the Father, Son, and Holy Spirit. Christ conquered death.

9 Pentecost.

Jesus ascended from the earth, but he did not leave the church powerless or alone. On the fiftieth day after the Jewish Passover (Pentecost means "fiftieth"), Jesus sent the Holy Spirit to create the church and take up residence among us. The Holy Spirit is present with us always.

10 The Second Coming.

One day, Christ will come again and end all suffering. This means that the final result of the epic battle between good and evil is already assured. It is simply that evil has not yet admitted defeat.

FOUR INSPIRING WOMEN OF THE BIBLE

Which heroine can inspire today's girl?

1 Esther (485–465 BCE):

She was a Jewish orphan in what is now Iran who risked her life to save the Jews from an ancient holocaust. She had intelligence and courage, both of which she used to save her people from the pogrom that faced them. The event is celebrated to this day in the festival of Purim.

2 Ruth (1100s BCE):

King David's great-grandmother started out as a destitute Arab widow and married an Israelite man showing that loyalty and love for your mother-in-law can help you out in the long run. She had the good sense to listen to someone older and wiser than herself, and most of us could learn a lot from her.

3 The Samaritan Woman (John 4:1–42):

She is not silent, and she is not limited to the private world of women. She has a voice, and she moves out into the public arena, into male space. She enters into debate with Jesus about issues and questions that interest her. She does not wait for permission to do so, but takes the initiative herself.

4 Priscilla (Acts 18:3):

Married to Aquila, they were tentmakers (or leather-workers). Notice the word "they." She was actively involved in the family business. They offered Paul work and shelter in their home as well when he came to Corinth. They were to be generous, loyal friends.

CALLED UP TO THE MAJORS (PROPHETS, THAT IS)

The terms "Major Prophets" and "Minor Prophets" are simply a way to divide the Old Testament prophetic books. The Major Prophets are Isaiah, Jeremiah, Lamentations, Ezekiel, and Daniel. The Minor Prophets are Hosea, Joel, Amos, Obadiah, Jonah, Micah, Nahum, Habakkuk, Zephaniah, Haggai, Zechariah, and Malachi.

The Major Prophets are described as "major" because their books are longer and the content is considered more important. The Minor Prophets are described as "minor" because their books are shorter (although Hosea and Zechariah are almost as long as Daniel) and the content is considered less important. That does not mean the Minor Prophets are any less inspired than the Major Prophets. It is simply a matter of God choosing to reveal more to the Major Prophets than He did to the Minor Prophets.

1 Isaiah:

Probably lived about 740–700 BCE, he is first mentioned in 2 Kings 19:2. The New Testament quotes him more than any other, about fifty times. He was a Jerusalem prophet who wrote like he knew Jesus as well as any disciple ever would. However, many scholars today believe there were two or three writers of this book of the Bible.

2 Jeremiah:

Born 640 BCE, he prophesied 627–586 BCE and is first mentioned in 2 Chronicles 35:25. He's known for trying to turn God down because of his age. When he wasn't prophesying doom and gloom you could find him in the potter's shed.

3 Lamentations:

Written at the time of the Fall of Judah in 586 BCE. This may not be the book to read if you're depressed, unless misery loves company. But it's the best place to go in the Bible if you want to understand how people feel when they've suffered indescribable loss.

4 Ezekiel:

He ministered from 593–571 BCE and offers us such bizarre behaviors that it's hard for us to forget his prophecies. He slept on his left side for 390 days and turned over to sleep on his right side for 40 days. He shaved his head and divided the hair into three piles. You'll have to read his book to figure out why.

5 Daniel:

A favorite of the younger set, he found himself in a variety of precarious situations for being firm in his faith—a fiery furnace and a lion's den. A good dream interpreter, he lived (600s–500s BCE) when the Jews were pondering a new teaching about the afterlife—resurrection.

THE TOP 10 BIBLE VILLAINS

❶ Satan

The Evil One is known by many names in the Bible and appears many places, but the devil's purpose is always the same: To disrupt and confuse people so they turn from God and seek to become their own gods. This Bible villain is still active today.

❷ The Serpent

In Eden, the serpent succeeded in tempting Eve to eat from the tree of the knowledge of good and evil (Genesis 3:1–7). As a result, sin entered creation. If it weren't for the serpent, we'd all still be walking around naked, eating fresh fruit, and living forever.

❸ Pharaoh (probably Seti I or Rameses II)

The notorious Pharaoh from the book of Exodus enslaved the Israelites. Moses eventually begged him to "let my people go," but Pharaoh hardened his heart and refused. Ten nasty plagues later, Pharaoh relented, but then changed his mind again. In the end, with his army at the bottom of the sea, Pharaoh finally gave his slaves up to the wilderness.

❹ Goliath

"The Philistine of Gath," who stood six cubits in height (about nine feet tall), was sent to fight David, still a downy-headed youth of fifteen. Goliath was a fighting champion known for killing people, but David drilled Goliath in the head with a rock from his sling and gave God the glory (1 Samuel 17).

one
cubit

Goliath   David

Though physically powerful, Goliath lost his battle with young David, one of the Top 10 heroes of the Bible.

⑤ Jezebel

King Ahab of Judah's wife and a follower of the false god Baal, Jezebel led her husband away from God and tried to kill off the prophets of the Lord. Elijah the prophet, however, was on the scene. He shamed Jezebel's false prophets and killed them (1 Kings 18:40).

⑥ King Herod

Afraid of any potential threat to his power, upon hearing about the birth of the Messiah in Bethlehem Herod sent the Wise Men to pinpoint his location. Awestruck by the Savior in the cradle, the Wise Men went home by a different route and avoided Herod. In a rage, he ordered the murder of every child two years of age or younger in the vicinity of Bethlehem. The baby Messiah escaped with his parents to Egypt (Matthew 2:14–15).

7 **The Pharisees, Sadducees, and Scribes**

They dogged Jesus throughout his ministry, alternately challenging his authority and being awed by his power. It was their leadership, with the consent and blessing of the people and the Roman government, that brought Jesus to trial and execution.

8 **Judas**

One of Jesus' original disciples, Judas earned 30 pieces of silver by betraying his Lord to the authorities. He accomplished this by leading the soldiers into the garden of Gethsemane where he revealed Jesus with a kiss (Matthew 26–27).

9 **Pontius Pilate**

The consummate politician, the Roman governor chose to preserve his own bloated status by giving the people what they wanted: Jesus' crucifixion. He washed his hands to signify self-absolution, but bloodied them instead.

10 **God's People**

They whine, they sin, they turn their backs on God over and over again. When given freedom, they blow it. When prophets preach to them, they stone them. When offered a Savior, we kill him. In the end, it must be admitted, God's people—us!—don't really shine. Only by God's grace and the gift of faith in Jesus Christ do we have hope.

THE TOP 10 BIBLE HEROES

The Bible is filled with typical examples of heroism, but another kind of hero inhabits the pages of the Bible—those people who, against all odds, follow God no matter the outcome. These are heroes of faith. You'll notice Jesus is not on this list—he's "above" all that.

❶ Noah

In the face of ridicule from others, Noah trusted God when God chose him to build an ark to save a remnant of humanity from destruction. Noah's trust became part of a covenant with God.

Noah trusted God, even though others made fun of him. By following God's instructions and building a great ark, Noah and his family survived the flood (Genesis 6–10).

❷ Abraham and Sarah

In extreme old age, Abraham and Sarah answered God's call to leave their home and travel to a strange land, where they became the parents of God's people.

❸ Moses

Moses, a man with a speech impediment, challenged the Egyptian powers to deliver God's people from bondage. He led a rebellious and contrary people for 40 years through the wilderness and gave them God's law.

4 Rahab

A prostitute who helped Israel conquer the Promised Land, Rahab was the great-grandmother of King David, and thus a part of the family of Jesus himself.

5 David

Great King David, the youngest and smallest member of his family, defeated great enemies, turning Israel into a world power. He wrote psalms, led armies, and confessed his sins to the Lord.

6 Mary and Joseph

These humble peasants responded to God's call to be the parents of the Messiah, although the call came through a pregnancy that was not the result of marriage.

7 The Canaanite Woman

Desperate for her daughter's health, the Canaanite woman challenged Jesus regarding women and race by claiming God's love for all people (Matthew 15:21–28). Because of this, Jesus praised her faith.

8 Peter

Peter was a man quick to speak but slow to think. At Jesus' trial, Peter denied ever having known him. But in the power of forgiveness and through Christ's appointment, Peter became a leader in the early church.

9 Saul/Paul

Originally an enemy and persecutor of Christians, Paul experienced a powerful vision of Jesus, converted, and became the greatest missionary the church has ever known.

10 Phoebe

A contemporary of Paul's, Phoebe is believed to have delivered the book of Romans after traveling some 800 miles from Cenchrea near Corinth to Rome. A wealthy woman, she used her influence to travel, protect other believers, and to host worship services in her home.

FIVE GROSS BIBLE STORIES FOR BOYS (AND GIRLS)

1 Eglon and Ehud (Judges 3:12–30)

Before kings reigned over Israel, judges ruled the people. At that time, a very overweight king named Eglon conquered Israel and demanded money. A man named Ehud brought the payment to Eglon while he was perched on his "throne" (meaning "toilet"). Along with the money, Ehud handed over a little something extra—his sword, which he buried so far in Eglon's belly that the sword disappeared into the king's fat and, as the Bible says, "the dirt came out" (v. 22).

2 Job's sores (Job 2:1–10)

Job lived a righteous life yet he suffered anyway. He had oozing sores from the bald spot on top of his head clear down to the soft spot on the bottom of his foot. Job used a broken piece of pottery to scrape away the pus that leaked from his sores.

3 The naked prophet (Isaiah 20)

God's prophets went to great lengths to get God's message across to the people. Isaiah was no exception. God's people planned a war, but God gave it the thumbs down. Isaiah marched around Jerusalem naked for three years as a sign of what would happen if the people went to war.

4 The almost-naked prophet (Jeremiah 13:1–11)

God sent Jeremiah to announce that God could no longer be proud of the people. To make the point, Jeremiah bought a new pair of underclothes, wore them every day without washing them, and then buried them in the wet river sand. Later, he dug them up, strapped them on, and shouted that this is what had happened to the people who were God's pride!

5 Spilling your guts (Matthew 27:1–8; Acts 1:16–19)

Judas betrayed Jesus and sold him out for 30 pieces of silver. He bought a field with the ill-gotten loot. Guilt-stricken, Judas walked out to the field, his belly swelled up until it burst, and his intestines spilled out onto the ground.

JESUS' FOURTEEN APOSTLES

While Jesus had many disciples (students and followers), the Bible focuses particularly on twelve who were closest to him. Tradition says that these twelve spread Jesus' message throughout the known world (Matthew 28:18–20). For this reason, they were known as "apostles," a word that means "sent ones." And then there are the replacements.

1 Andrew

A fisherman and the first disciple to follow Jesus, Andrew brought his brother, Simon Peter, to Jesus.

2 Bartholomew

Also called Nathanael, tradition has it that he was martyred by being skinned alive.

3 James the Elder

James, with John and Peter, was one of Jesus' closest disciples. Herod Agrippa killed James because of his faith, which made him a martyr (Acts 12:2).

4 John

John (or one of his followers) is thought to be the author of the Gospel of John and three letters of John. He probably died of natural causes in old age.

5 Matthew

Matthew was a tax collector and, therefore, probably an outcast even among his own people. He is attributed with the authorship of the Gospel of Matthew.

6 Peter

Peter was a fisherman who was brought to faith by his brother Andrew. He was probably martyred in Rome by being crucified upside-down.

7 Philip

Philip, possibly a Greek, is responsible for bringing Bartholomew (Nathanael) to faith. He is thought to have died in a city called Phrygia.

8 James the Less

James was called "the Less" so he wouldn't be confused with James, the brother of John, or James, Jesus' brother.

9 Simon

Simon is often called "the Zealot." Zealots were a political group in Jesus' day that favored the overthrow of the Roman government by force.

10 Jude

Jude may have worked with Simon the Zealot in Persia (Iran) where they were martyred on the same day.

11 Thomas

"Doubting" Thomas preached the message of Jesus in India.

12 Judas Iscariot

Judas was the treasurer for Jesus' disciples and the one who betrayed Jesus for 30 pieces of silver. According to the Bible, Judas killed himself for his betrayal.

13 Matthias

Matthias was chosen by lot to replace Judas. It is thought that he worked mostly in Ethiopia.

14 Paul

Paul is considered primarily responsible for bringing non-Jewish people to faith in Jesus. He traveled extensively and wrote many letters to believers. Many of Paul's letters are included in the New Testament.

THE THREE MOST REBELLIOUS THINGS JESUS DID

1 The prophet returned to his hometown.
(Luke 4:14–27)

Jesus returned to Nazareth, where he was raised, and was invited to read Scripture and preach. First, he insisted that the scriptures he read were not just comforting promises of a distant future, but that they were about him, local boy, anointed by God. Second, he insisted God would bless foreigners with those same promises through him. These statements amounted to the unpardonable crime of blasphemy!

2 The rebel thumbed his nose at the authorities.
(John 11:55–12:11)

Jesus had become an outlaw, hunted by the religious authorities who wanted to kill him. Mary, Martha, and Lazarus threw a thank-you party for Jesus in Bethany, right outside Jerusalem, the authorities' stronghold. In spite of the threats to his life, Jesus went to the party. This was not just rebellion but a demonstration of how much Jesus loved his friends.

3 The king rode a royal procession right under Caesar's nose
(Matthew 21:1–17; Mark 11:1–10; Luke 19:28–38; John 12:12–19)

Jesus entered Jerusalem during a great festival, in full view of adoring crowds, as a king comes home to rule. Riding the colt, heralded by the people with cloaks and branches, accompanied by the royal anthem (Psalm 118), he rode in to claim Jerusalem for God and himself as God's anointed. The Roman overlords and the Jewish leaders watched this seditious act and prepared for a crucifixion.

MAPS, DIAGRAMS, AND CHARTS

THE EXODUS

MEDITERRANEAN SEA

The promised land.

The exodus began here.

Lake Galilee

Jordan River

Mount Nebo

NILE DELTA

Jericho
Jerusalem ●
Gaza ● Hebron ●
Beersheba ●

DEAD SEA

Rameses
GOSHEN
Succoth

Zamorrah

ZIN DESERT

Kadesh-Barnea

MOAB

SHUR DESERT

Heliopolis ●
Pi-Hahiroth
● Memphis

SINAI PENNISULA

Jothathah

EGYPT

PARAN DESERT

EDOM

Heracleopolis ●

Marah
Elim

SIN DESERT

Ezion-Geber

Hazepoth

MIDIAN

NILE RIVER

Gulf of Suez

Gulf of Aqabah

Mount Sinai

● Akhetaton

RED SEA

Abydos ●

God led the Israelites out of slavery in Egypt, through the wilderness, and to the promised land. Here is one possible route they took.

THE ARK OF THE COVENANT

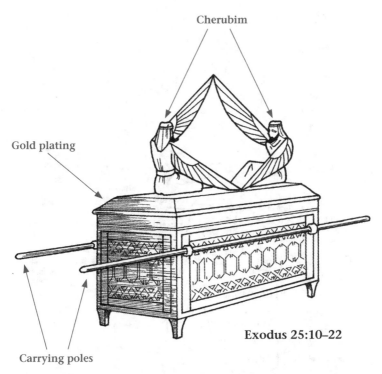

Cherubim

Gold plating

Carrying poles

Exodus 25:10–22

God told the Israelites to place the stone tablets—the "covenant"—of the law into the Ark of the Covenant. The Israelites believed that God was invisibly enthroned above the vessel and went before them wherever they traveled.

The Ark of the Covenant was 2.5 cubits long and 1.5 cubits wide (Exodus 25:17).

JERUSALEM IN JESUS' TIME

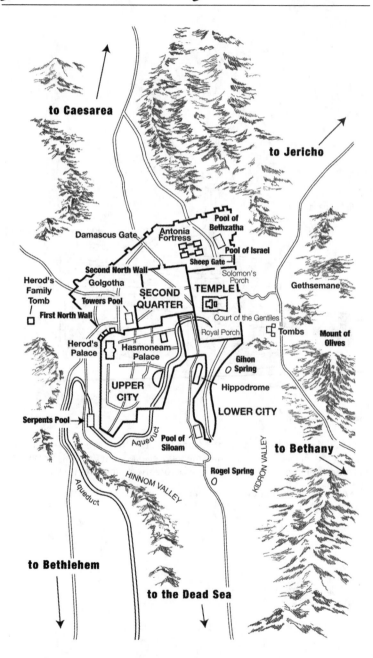

to Caesarea

to Jericho

Pool of
Bethzatha

Damascus Gate

Antonia
Fortress

Pool of Israel

Second North Wall

Sheep Gate

Solomon's
Porch

Herod's
Family
Tomb

Golgotha

SECOND
QUARTER

TEMPLE

Gethsemane

Towers Pool

Court of the Gentiles

First North Wall

Royal Porch

Tombs

Mount of
Olives

Herod's
Palace

Hasmoneam
Palace

Gihon
Spring

UPPER
CITY

Hippodrome

LOWER CITY

Serpents Pool

Aqueduct

Pool of
Siloam

to Bethany

HINNOM VALLEY

Rogel Spring

KIDRON VALLEY

to Bethlehem

Aqueduct

to the Dead Sea

THE PASSION AND CRUCIFIXION

Judas betrayed Jesus with a kiss, saying, "The one I will kiss is the man; arrest him" (Matthew 26:48).

Peter denied Jesus three times (Matthew 26:69–75).

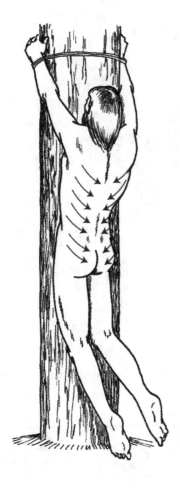

Jesus was flogged as part of his punishment. The pain would have been unbearable (Matthew 26:67).

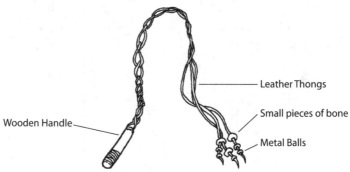

Wooden Handle

Leather Thongs

Small pieces of bone

Metal Balls

Whip used for flogging

After being flogged, carrying the patibulum was nearly impossible for Jesus.

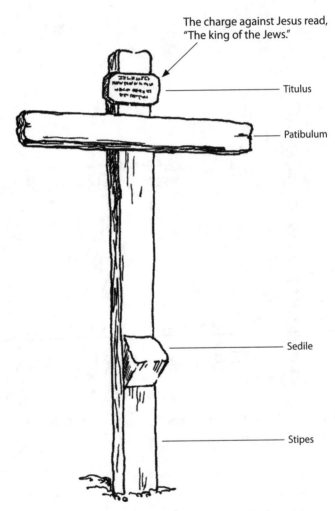

The charge against Jesus read, "The king of the Jews."

Titulus

Patibulum

Sedile

Stipes

Crucifixion was so common in Jesus' time that the Romans had special names for the parts of the cross.

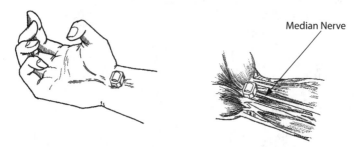

Median Nerve

Typical crucifixion involved being nailed to the cross through the wrists—an excruciatingly painful and humiliating punishment.

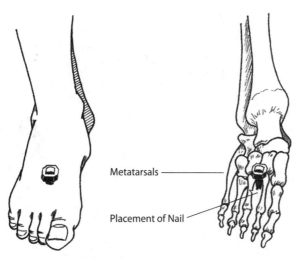

Metatarsals

Placement of Nail

During a crucifixion, a single nail usually was used to pin both feet together to the cross.

Eventually, the victim would be unable to lift himself to take a breath, and he would suffocate.

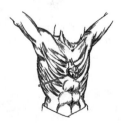

While the Romans broke the legs of the men who were crucified next to Jesus, they found that Jesus had already died. To make sure, they pierced his side with a spear, probably to puncture his heart (John 19:34).

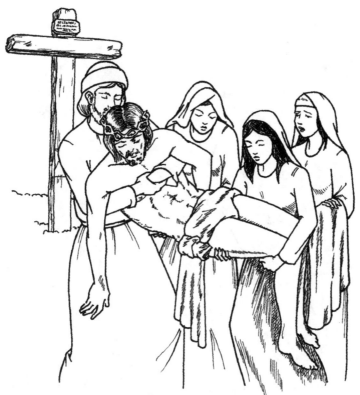

Joseph of Arimathea and several women took Jesus down and carried him to the tomb (Matthew 27:57–61).

The miracle of resurrection took place three days later, when Jesus rose from the dead.

FAMILY TREE
OF CHRISTIANITY

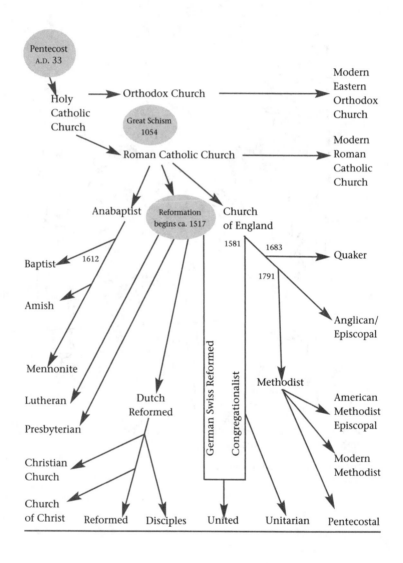

EPISCOSPEAK

Impress your friends by using any of these words in a conversation

Alb. A long white garment with narrow sleeves, which is the basic garment worn by ordained and lay ministers (including Christian educators) at the Eucharist and at other church services.

Alleluia. A liturgical expression of praise, "Praise ye the Lord," from the Hebrew *Hallelujah.* Alleluia is not said during Lent.

Altar. The structure, also known as "the Lord's Table," "the Holy Table," and "the Table," where the offerings are presented and the elements of bread and wine are consecrated at the Eucharist.

Altar Guild. A volunteer group in the church whose ministry is to care for the altar, vestments, vessels, and altar linens of the parish. They sometimes arrange flowers, too.

Annual Meeting. A meeting of members of a congregation, parish, or mission typically held to elect vestry members and review reports from staff and committees, as well as discuss by-laws and budget.

Baptism. Full initiation by water and the Holy Spirit into Christ's Body, the church. In the Episcopal Church it makes one a full member, no matter their age or anything else.

Baptismal Covenant. The rite of Christian initiation contains a series of vows, made by all present. In the Episcopal Church it is widely regarded as the normative statement of what it means to follow Christ. It is the curriculum!

BCP. The Book of Common Prayer for short. We love our acronyms.

Bishop. One of three orders of ordained ministers in the church, they represent Christ and his church, and they are called to provide Christian vision and leadership for their dioceses, elected by clergy and lay members of that diocese.

Canon. 1.) The canon of scripture is the list of inspired books recognized by the church to constitute the Holy Scriptures. 2.) Canons are the written rules that provide a code of laws for the governance of the church, enacted by General Convention.

3.) A canon may be the title of a staff person associated with a diocese or cathedral.

Catechesis. Systematic instruction and formation of adults for baptism, initiating them into the mysteries and life of the Christian faith.

Catechist. A teacher, lay or ordained, who provides instruction in the Christian faith.

Catechumenate. An organized time of Christian formation and education in preparation for baptism.

Cathedral. A church that contains the diocesan bishop's "seat" and may serve as the symbol and center of diocesan ministry. The dean is the clergyperson with pastoral charge of the cathedral.

Chalice. The cup for the wine that is consecrated and administered at the Eucharist.

Confirmation. The rite in which candidates "express a mature commitment to Christ, and receive strength from the Holy Spirit through prayer and the laying on of hands by a bishop." (BCP p. 860)

Creed. A concise and formal statement of basic beliefs about God, derived from the Latin *credo*, "I believe."

Deacon. One of three distinct orders of ordained ministry, a deacon exercises "a special ministry of servanthood," serving all people and especially those in need. (BCP p. 543)

Disciple. A follower or pupil of a great master.

Doctrine. From Latin *docere*, "to teach," in a theological context carries the implication of belonging to a school of thought or body of believers.

Dogma. Definitive teaching of the church, which is to be believed by the members of the church, from the Greek *dokein*, "to seem."

Domestic and Foreign Missionary Society. (DFMS) The full legal name of the corporate body of the Episcopal Church.

Ecumenical. Referring to the wholeness of the church.

Enriching Our Worship. A collection of liturgical materials to supplement the Book of Common Prayer.

Episcopal Church Center. The headquarters for the Episcopal Church, currently located at 815 Second Avenue in New York City. Aka "815."

Episcopal Youth Event. (EYE) A church-wide gathering of high school young people and adult sponsors from throughout the Episcopal Church that occurs every three years.

Eucharist. The sacrament of Christ's body and blood and the principal act of Christian worship. The term is from the Greek, "thanksgiving."

General Convention. The church-wide legislative body of the Episcopal Church consisting of a House of Bishops (all bishops, active and retired) and a House of Deputies (four lay persons and four clergy from each diocese) that meets every three years.

Inclusive Language. Spoken and written language that intentionally avoids word use that is needlessly gender-specific or exclusive.

Inquirers' Class. Class for newcomers or visitors who "inquire" about the Episcopal Church.

Lay Ministry. The term refers to the many ways the laity (non-ordained) of the church live out their baptismal covenant.

Lectern. A book stand or reading desk that holds the book for reading scripture in public worship. It may also be used for preaching the Word, or a sermon.

Liturgy. The church's public worship of God. The term is derived from Greek words for "people" and "work."

Mission. From the Latin "to send." Christian mission is the sending forth to proclaim the gospel of Jesus Christ.

Mutual Ministry. A term given to the concept of shared ministry and leadership in a congregation, with all members living out promises made at baptism as the doers of ministry within and beyond the congregation.

Narthex. An entry space, foyer, or anteroom of a church between the door and the nave (congregational worship space).

Parish. A self-supporting congregation with a rector.

Paten. A shallow dish or small plate for the bread at the Eucharist.

Pilgrim. One who goes on a pilgrimage or journey with a religious or devotional intention.

Presiding Bishop. Chief Pastor and Primate of the Episcopal Church, elected every nine years at General Convention.

Priest. Derived from the Greek *presbyteros*, "elder," or "old man," in the Episcopal Church his or her role is "to represent Christ and his Church, particularly as pastor to the people; to share with the bishop in the overseeing of the Church; to proclaim the Gospel; to administer the sacraments; and to bless and declare pardon in the name of God." (BCP p. 856)

Province. The Episcopal Church is divided into nine provinces (regions), each with a synod consisting of bishops, clergy, and laypersons.

Rector. A priest "in charge" of a self-supporting parish or congregation. He or she may live in a rectory, which is owned by the church.

Rite I. Rite II. The 1979 BCP provides the services of Morning Prayer, Evening Prayer, the Holy Eucharist and the Burial Office in both traditional (I) and contemporary (II) language.

Sacrament. An outward and visible sign of inward and spiritual grace, given by Christ as sure and certain means of receiving God's grace. In the Episcopal Church, Baptism and Eucharist are the two great sacraments.

Sacristy. The room adjoining a church where vestments, altar hangings, sacred vessels and liturgical elements are kept until needed for worship. This is where you'll find the altar guild at work.

Spiritual Director. A person, lay or ordained, with whom one communicates concerning the spiritual life; may also be known as a soul-friend, soul-mate, or spiritual companion.

Undercroft. A large room or area beneath a church building. It may be used as a space for prayer, church meetings, Christian education classes, or other church purposes.

Vestry. The legal representatives of the parish with regard to all matters pertaining to its corporate property. Their main responsibilities are to help define and articulate the mission of the congregation. Vestry members are usually elected at the annual parish meeting.

Vicar. A priest-in-charge of a mission congregation.

Warden. In a church context, these are the officers of a parish. Two are generally elected ("senior" and "junior") at the annual parish meeting.

EXTRA IMPORTANT STUFF

THE LORD'S PRAYER
(from The Book of Common Prayer, page 364)

Traditional

Our Father, who art in heaven,
  hallowed be thy Name,
  thy kingdom come,
  thy will be done,
    on earth as it is in heaven.
Give us this day our daily bread.
And forgive us our trespasses,
  as we forgive those
    who trespass against us.
And lead us not into temptation,
  but deliver us from evil.
For thine is the kingdom,
  and the power, and
    the glory,
  for ever and ever. Amen.

Contemporary

Our Father in heaven,
  hallowed be your Name,
  your kingdom come,
  your will be done,
    on earth as in heaven.
Give us today our daily bread.
Forgive us our sins
  as we forgive those
    who sin against us.
Save us from the time of trial,
  and deliver us from evil.
For the kingdom, the power,
  and the glory are yours,
  now and for ever. Amen.

THE TEN COMMANDMENTS

(from The Book of Common Prayer, page 350)

Hear the commandments of God to his people:
I am the Lord your God who brought you out of bondage.
You shall have no other gods but me.
Amen. Lord have mercy.

You shall not make for yourself any idol.
Amen. Lord have mercy.

You shall not invoke with malice the Name of the Lord your God.
Amen. Lord have mercy.

Remember the Sabbath Day and keep it holy.
Amen. Lord have mercy.

Honor your father and your mother.
Amen. Lord have mercy.

You shall not commit murder.
Amen. Lord have mercy.

You shall not commit adultery.
Amen. Lord have mercy.

You shall not steal.
Amen. Lord have mercy.

You shall not be a false witness.
Amen. Lord have mercy.

You shall not covet anything that belongs to your neighbor.
Amen. Lord have mercy.

THE BAPTISMAL COVENANT
(from The Book of Common Prayer, page 304)

Celebrant Do you believe in God the Father?

People I believe in God, the Father almighty,
creator of heaven and earth.

Celebrant Do you believe in Jesus Christ, the Son of God?

People I believe in Jesus Christ, his only Son, our Lord.
He was conceived by the power of the
Holy Spirit and born of the Virgin Mary.
He suffered under Pontius Pilate,
was crucified, died, and was buried.
He descended to the dead.
On the third day he rose again.
He ascended into heaven,
and is seated at the right hand of the Father.
He will come again to judge the living and
the dead.

Celebrant Do you believe in God the Holy Spirit?

People I believe in the Holy Spirit,
the holy catholic Church,
the communion of saints,
the forgiveness of sins,
the resurrection of the body,
and the life everlasting.

Celebrant Will you continue in the apostles' teaching and fellowship, in the breaking of bread, and in the prayers?

People I will, with God's help.

Celebrant Will you persevere in resisting evil, and, whenever you
fall into sin, repent and return to the Lord?

People I will, with God's help.

Celebrant Will you proclaim by word and example the Good
News of God in Christ?

People I will, with God's help.

Celebrant Will you seek and serve Christ in all persons, loving your neighbor as yourself?

People I will, with God's help.

Celebrant Will you strive for justice and peace among all people, and respect the dignity of every human being?

People I will, with God's help.

AN OUTLINE OF THE FAITH

COMMONLY CALLED THE CATECHISM

(from The Book of Common Prayer, pages 845–862)

Human Nature

Q. What are we by nature?

A. We are part of God's creation, made in the image of God.

Q. What does it mean to be created in the image of God?

A. It means that we are free to make choices: to love, to create, to reason, and to live in harmony with creation and with God.

Q. Why then do we live apart from God and out of harmony with creation?

A. From the beginning, human beings have misused their freedom and made wrong choices.

Q. Why do we not use our freedom as we should?

A. Because we rebel against God, and we put ourselves in the place of God.

Q. What help is there for us?

A. Our help is in God.

Q. How did God first help us?

A. God first helped us by revealing himself and his will, through nature and history, through many seers and saints, and especially through the prophets of Israel.

God the Father

Q. What do we learn about God as creator from the revelation to Israel?

A. We learn that there is one God, the Father Almighty, creator of heaven and earth, of all that is, seen and unseen.

Q. What does this mean?

A. This means that the universe is good, that it is the work of a single loving God who creates, sustains, and directs it.

Q. What does this mean about our place in the universe?

A. It means that the world belongs to its creator; and that we are called to enjoy it and to care for it in accordance with God's purposes.

Q. What does this mean about human life?

A. It means that all people are worthy of respect and honor, because all are created in the image of God, and all can respond to the love of God.

Q. How was this revelation handed down to us?

A. This revelation was handed down to us through a community created by a covenant with God.

The Old Covenant

Q. What is meant by a covenant with God?

A. A covenant is a relationship initiated by God, to which a body of people responds in faith.

Q. What is the Old Covenant?

A. The Old Covenant is the one given by God to the Hebrew people.

Q. What did God promise them?

A. God promised that they would be his people to bring all the nations of the world to him.

Q. What response did God require from the chosen people?

A. God required the chosen people to be faithful; to love justice, to do mercy, and to walk humbly with their God.

Q. Where is this Old Covenant to be found?

A. The covenant with the Hebrew people is to be found in the books which we call the Old Testament.

Q. Where in the Old Testament is God's will for us shown most clearly?

A. God's will for us is shown most clearly in the Ten Commandments.

The Ten Commandments

Q. What are the Ten Commandments?

A. The Ten Commandments are the laws given to Moses and the people of Israel.

Q. What do we learn from these commandments?

A. We learn two things: our duty to God, and our duty to our neighbors.

Q. What is our duty to God?

A. Our duty is to believe and trust in God;

    I To love and obey God and to bring others to know him;

    II To put nothing in the place of God;

    III To show God respect in thought, word, and deed;

    IV And to set aside regular times for worship, prayer, and the study of God's ways.

Q. What is our duty to our neighbors?

A. Our duty to our neighbors is to love them as ourselves, and to do to other people as we wish them to do to us;

    V To love, honor, and help our parents and family; to honor those in authority, and to meet their just demands;

    VI To show respect for the life God has given us; to work and pray for peace; to bear no malice, prejudice, or hatred in our hearts; and to be kind to all the creatures of God;

    VII To use all our bodily desires as God intended;

    VIII To be honest and fair in our dealings; to seek justice, freedom, and the necessities of life for all people; and to use our talents and possessions as ones who must answer for them to God;

    IX To speak the truth, and not to mislead others by our silence;

    X To resist temptations to envy, greed, and jealousy; to rejoice in other people's gifts and graces; and to do our duty for the love of God, who has called us into fellowship with him.

Q. What is the purpose of the Ten Commandments?

A. The Ten Commandments were given to define our relationship with God and our neighbors.

Q. Since we do not fully obey them, are they useful at all?

A. Since we do not fully obey them, we see more clearly our sin and our need for redemption.

Sin and Redemption

Q. What is sin?

A. Sin is the seeking of our own will instead of the will of God, thus distorting our relationship with God, with other people, and with all creation.

Q. How does sin have power over us?

A. Sin has power over us because we lose our liberty when our relationship with God is distorted.

Q. What is redemption?

A. Redemption is the act of God which sets us free from the power of evil, sin, and death.

Q. How did God prepare us for redemption?

A. God sent the prophets to call us back to himself, to show us our need for redemption, and to announce the coming of the Messiah.

Q. What is meant by the Messiah?

A. The Messiah is one sent by God to free us from the power of sin, so that with the help of God we may live in harmony with God, within ourselves, with our neighbors, and with all creation.

Q. Who do we believe is the Messiah?

A. The Messiah, or Christ, is Jesus of Nazareth, the only Son of God.

God the Son

Q. What do we mean when we say that Jesus is the only Son of God?

A. We mean that Jesus is the only perfect image of the Father, and shows us the nature of God.

Q. What is the nature of God revealed in Jesus?

A. God is love.

Q. What do we mean when we say that Jesus was conceived by the power of the Holy Spirit and became incarnate from the Virgin Mary?

A. We mean that by God's own act, his divine Son received our human nature from the Virgin Mary, his mother.

Q. Why did he take our human nature?

A. The divine Son became human, so that in him human beings might be adopted as children of God, and be made heirs of God's kingdom.

Q. What is the great importance of Jesus' suffering and death?

A. By his obedience, even to suffering and death, Jesus made the offering which we could not make; in him we are freed from the power of sin and reconciled to God.

Q. What is the significance of Jesus' resurrection?

A. By his resurrection, Jesus overcame death and opened for us the way of eternal life.

Q. What do we mean when we say that he descended to the dead?

A. We mean that he went to the departed and offered them also the benefits of redemption.

Q. What do we mean when we say that he ascended into heaven and is seated at the right hand of the Father?

A. We mean that Jesus took our human nature into heaven where he now reigns with the Father and intercedes for us.

Q. How can we share in his victory over sin, suffering, and death?

A. We share in his victory when we are baptized into the New Covenant and become living members of Christ.

The New Covenant

Q. What is the New Covenant?

A. The New Covenant is the new relationship with God given by Jesus Christ, the Messiah, to the apostles; and, through them, to all who believe in him.

Q. What did the Messiah promise in the New Covenant?

A. Christ promised to bring us into the kingdom of God and give us life in all its fullness.

Q. What response did Christ require?

A. Christ commanded us to believe in him and to keep his commandments.

Q. What are the commandments taught by Christ?

A. Christ taught us the Summary of the Law and gave us the New Commandment.

Q. What is the Summary of the Law?

A. You shall love the Lord your God with all your heart, with all your soul, and with all your mind. This is the first and the great commandment. And the second is like it: You shall love your neighbor as yourself.

Q. What is the New Commandment?

A. The New Commandment is that we love one another as Christ loved us.

Q. Where may we find what Christians believe about Christ?

A. What Christians believe about Christ is found in the Scriptures and summed up in the creeds.

The Creeds

Q. What are the creeds?

A. The creeds are statements of our basic beliefs about God.

Q. How many creeds does this Church use in its worship?

A. This Church uses two creeds: The Apostles' Creed and the Nicene Creed.

Q. What is the Apostles' Creed?

A. The Apostles' Creed is the ancient creed of Baptism; it is used in the Church's daily worship to recall our Baptismal Covenant.

Q. What is the Nicene Creed?

A. The Nicene Creed is the creed of the universal Church and is used at the Eucharist.

Q. What, then, is the Athanasian Creed?

A. The Athanasian Creed is an ancient document proclaiming the nature of the Incarnation and of God as Trinity.

Q. What is the Trinity?

A. The Trinity is one God: Father, Son, and Holy Spirit.

The Holy Spirit

Q. Who is the Holy Spirit?

A. The Holy Spirit is the Third Person of the Trinity, God at work in the world and in the Church even now.

Q. How is the Holy Spirit revealed in the Old Covenant?

A. The Holy Spirit is revealed in the Old Covenant as the giver of life, the One who spoke through the prophets.

Q. How is the Holy Spirit revealed in the New Covenant?

A. The Holy Spirit is revealed as the Lord who leads us into all truth and enables us to grow in the likeness of Christ.

Q. How do we recognize the presence of the Holy Spirit in our lives?

A. We recognize the presence of the Holy Spirit when we confess Jesus Christ as Lord and are brought into love and harmony with God, with ourselves, with our neighbors, and with all creation.

Q. How do we recognize the truths taught by the Holy Spirit?

A. We recognize truths to be taught by the Holy Spirit when they are in accord with the Scriptures.

The Holy Scriptures

Q. What are the Holy Scriptures?

A. The Holy Scriptures, commonly called the Bible, are the books of the Old and New Testaments; other books, called the Apocrypha, are often included in the Bible.

Q. What is the Old Testament?

A. The Old Testament consists of books written by the people of the Old Covenant, under the inspiration of the Holy Spirit, to show God at work in nature and history.

Q. What is the New Testament?

A. The New Testament consists of books written by the people of the New Covenant, under the inspiration of the Holy Spirit, to set forth the life and teachings of Jesus and to proclaim the Good News of the Kingdom for all people.

Q. What is the Apocrypha?

A. The Apocrypha is a collection of additional books written by people of the Old Covenant, and used in the Christian Church.

Q. Why do we call the Holy Scriptures the Word of God?

A. We call them the Word of God because God inspired their human authors and because God still speaks to us through the Bible.

Q. How do we understand the meaning of the Bible?

A. We understand the meaning of the Bible by the help of the Holy Spirit, who guides the Church in the true interpretation of the Scriptures.

The Church

Q. What is the Church?

A. The Church is the community of the New Covenant.

Q. How is the Church described in the Bible?

A. The Church is described as the Body of which Jesus Christ is the Head and of which all baptized persons are members. It is called the People of God, the New Israel, a holy nation, a royal priesthood, and the pillar and ground of truth.

Q. How is the Church described in the creeds?

A. The Church is described as one, holy, catholic, and apostolic.

Q. Why is the Church described as one?

A. The Church is one, because it is one Body, under one Head, our Lord Jesus Christ.

Q. Why is the Church described as holy?

A. The Church is holy, because the Holy Spirit dwells in it, consecrates its members, and guides them to do God's work.

Q. Why is the Church described as catholic?

A. The Church is catholic, because it proclaims the whole Faith to all people, to the end of time.

Q. Why is the Church described as apostolic?

A. The Church is apostolic, because it continues in the teaching and fellowship of the apostles and is sent to carry out Christ's mission to all people.

Q. What is the mission of the Church?

A. The mission of the Church is to restore all people to unity with God and each other in Christ.

Q. How does the Church pursue its mission?

A. The Church pursues its mission as it prays and worships, proclaims the Gospel, and promotes justice, peace, and love.

Q. Through whom does the Church carry out its mission?

A. The Church carries out its mission through the ministry of all its members.

The Ministry

Q. Who are the ministers of the Church?

A. The ministers of the Church are lay persons, bishops, priests, and deacons.

Q. What is the ministry of the laity?

A. The ministry of lay persons is to represent Christ and his Church; to bear witness to him wherever they may be and, according to the gifts given them, to carry on Christ's work of reconciliation in the world; and to take their place in the life, worship, and governance of the Church.

Q. What is the ministry of a bishop?

A. The ministry of a bishop is to represent Christ and his Church, particularly as apostle, chief priest, and pastor of a diocese; to guard the faith, unity, and discipline of the whole Church; to proclaim the Word of God; to act in Christ's name for the reconciliation of the world and the building up of the Church; and to ordain others to continue Christ's ministry.

Q. What is the ministry of a priest or presbyter?

A. The ministry of a priest is to represent Christ and his Church, particularly as pastor to the people; to share with the bishop in the overseeing of the Church; to proclaim the Gospel; to administer the sacraments; and to bless and declare pardon in the name of God.

Q. What is the ministry of a deacon?

A. The ministry of a deacon is to represent Christ and his Church, particularly as a servant of those in need; and to assist bishops and priests in the proclamation of the Gospel and the administration of the sacraments.

Q. What is the duty of all Christians?

A. The duty of all Christians is to follow Christ; to come together week by week for corporate worship; and to work, pray, and give for the spread of the kingdom of God.

Prayer and Worship

Q. What is prayer?

A. Prayer is responding to God, by thought and by deeds, with or without words.

Q. What is Christian Prayer?

A. Christian prayer is response to God the Father, through Jesus Christ, in the power of the Holy Spirit.

Q. What prayer did Christ teach us?

A. Our Lord gave us the example of prayer known as the Lord's Prayer.

Q. What are the principal kinds of prayer?

A. The principal kinds of prayer are adoration, praise, thanksgiving, penitence, oblation, intercession, and petition.

Q. What is adoration?

A. Adoration is the lifting up of the heart and mind to God, asking nothing but to enjoy God's presence.

Q. Why do we praise God?

A. We praise God, not to obtain anything, but because God's Being draws praise from us.

Q. For what do we offer thanksgiving?

A. Thanksgiving is offered to God for all the blessings of this life, for our redemption, and for whatever draws us closer to God.

Q. What is penitence?

A. In penitence, we confess our sins and make restitution where possible, with the intention to amend our lives.

Q. What is prayer of oblation?

A. Oblation is an offering of ourselves, our lives and labors, in union with Christ, for the purposes of God.

Q. What are intercession and petition?

A. Intercession brings before God the needs of others; in petition, we present our own needs, that God's will may be done.

Q. What is corporate worship?

A. In corporate worship, we unite ourselves with others to acknowledge the holiness of God, to hear God's Word, to offer prayer, and to celebrate the sacraments.

The Sacraments

Q. What are the sacraments?

A. The sacraments are outward and visible signs of inward and spiritual grace, given by Christ as sure and certain means by which we receive that grace.

Q. What is grace?

A. Grace is God's favor towards us, unearned and undeserved; by grace God forgives our sins, enlightens our minds, stirs our hearts, and strengthens our wills.

Q. What are the two great sacraments of the Gospel?

A. The two great sacraments given by Christ to his Church are Holy Baptism and the Holy Eucharist.

Holy Baptism

Q. What is Holy Baptism?

A. Holy Baptism is the sacrament by which God adopts us as his children and makes us members of Christ's Body, the Church, and inheritors of the kingdom of God.

Q. What is the outward and visible sign in Baptism?

A. The outward and visible sign in Baptism is water, in which the person is baptized in the Name of the Father, and of the Son, and of the Holy Spirit.

Q. What is the inward and spiritual grace in Baptism?

A. The inward and spiritual grace in Baptism is union with Christ in his death and resurrection, birth into God's family the Church, forgiveness of sins, and new life in the Holy Spirit.

Q. What is required of us at Baptism?

A. It is required that we renounce Satan, repent of our sins, and accept Jesus as our Lord and Savior.

Q. Why then are infants baptized?

A. Infants are baptized so that they can share citizenship in the Covenant, membership in Christ, and redemption by God.

Q. How are the promises for infants made and carried out?

A. Promises are made for them by their parents and sponsors, who guarantee that the infants will be brought up within the Church, to know Christ and be able to follow him.

The Holy Eucharist

Q. What is the Holy Eucharist?

A. The Holy Eucharist is the sacrament commanded by Christ for the continual remembrance of his life, death, and resurrection, until his coming again.

Q. Why is the Eucharist called a sacrifice?

A. Because the Eucharist, the Church's sacrifice of praise and thanksgiving, is the way by which the sacrifice of Christ is made present, and in which he unites us to his one offering of himself.

Q. By what other names is this service known?

A. The Holy Eucharist is called the Lord's Supper, and Holy Communion; it is also known as the Divine Liturgy, the Mass, and the Great Offering.

Q. What is the outward and visible sign in the Eucharist?

A. The outward and visible sign in the Eucharist is bread and wine, given and received according to Christ's command.

Q. What is the inward and spiritual grace given in the Eucharist?

A. The inward and spiritual grace in the Holy Communion is the Body and Blood of Christ given to his people, and received by faith.

Q. What are the benefits which we receive in the Lord's Supper?

A. The benefits we receive are the forgiveness of our sins, the strengthening of our union with Christ and one another, and the foretaste of the heavenly banquet which is our nourishment in eternal life.

Q. What is required of us when we come to the Eucharist?

A. It is required that we should examine our lives, repent of our sins, and be in love and charity with all people.

Other Sacramental Rites

Q. What other sacramental rites evolved in the Church under the guidance of the Holy Spirit?

A. Other sacramental rites which evolved in the Church include confirmation, ordination, holy matrimony, reconciliation of a penitent, and unction.

Q. How do they differ from the two sacraments of the Gospel?

A. Although they are means of grace, they are not necessary for all persons in the same way that Baptism and the Eucharist are.

Q. What is Confirmation?

A. Confirmation is the rite in which we express a mature commitment to Christ, and receive strength from the Holy Spirit through prayer and the laying on of hands by a bishop.

Q. What is required of those to be confirmed?

A. It is required of those to be confirmed that they have been baptized, are sufficiently instructed in the Christian Faith, are penitent for their sins, and are ready to affirm their confession of Jesus Christ as Savior and Lord.

Q. What is Ordination?

A. Ordination is the rite in which God gives authority and the grace of the Holy Spirit to those being made bishops, priests, and deacons, through prayer and the laying on of hands by bishops.

Q. What is Holy Matrimony?

A. Holy Matrimony is Christian marriage, in which the woman and man enter into a life-long union, make their vows before God and the Church, and receive the grace and blessing of God to help them fulfill their vows.

Q. What is Reconciliation of a Penitent?

A. Reconciliation of a Penitent, or Penance, is the rite in which those who repent of their sins may confess them to God in the presence of a priest, and receive the assurance of pardon and the grace of absolution.

Q. What is Unction of the Sick?

A. Unction is the rite of anointing the sick with oil, or the laying on of hands, by which God's grace is given for the healing of spirit, mind, and body.

Q. Is God's activity limited to these rites?

A. God does not limit himself to these rites; they are patterns of countless ways by which God uses material things to reach out to us.

Q. How are the sacraments related to our Christian hope?

A. Sacraments sustain our present hope and anticipate its future fulfillment.

The Christian Hope

Q. What is the Christian hope?

A. The Christian hope is to live with confidence in newness and fullness of life, and to await the coming of Christ in glory, and the completion of God's purpose for the world.

Q. What do we mean by the coming of Christ in glory?

A. By the coming of Christ in glory, we mean that Christ will come, not in weakness but in power, and will make all things new.

Q. What do we mean by heaven and hell?

A. By heaven, we mean eternal life in our enjoyment of God; by hell, we mean eternal death in our rejection of God.

Q. Why do we pray for the dead?

A. We pray for them, because we still hold them in our love, and because we trust that in God's presence those who have chosen to serve him will grow in his love, until they see him as he is.

Q. What do we mean by the last judgment?

A. We believe that Christ will come in glory and judge the living and the dead.

Q. What do we mean by the resurrection of the body?

A. We mean that God will raise us from death in the fullness of our being, that we may live with Christ in the communion of the saints.

Q. What is the communion of saints?

A. The communion of saints is the whole family of God, the living and the dead, those whom we love and those whom we hurt, bound together in Christ by sacrament, prayer, and praise.

Q. What do we mean by everlasting life?

A. By everlasting life, we mean a new existence, in which we are united with all the people of God, in the joy of fully knowing and loving God and each other.

Q. What, then, is our assurance as Christians?

A. Our assurance as Christians is that nothing, not even death, shall separate us from the love of God which is in Christ Jesus our Lord. Amen.

A CHILDREN'S CHARTER
FOR THE CHURCH

General Convention accepted a resolution (1997-B005) for all congregations to consider their ministry with children through the mandate of A Children's Charter for the Church.

Nurture of the Child

Children are a heritage from the LORD, and the fruit of the womb is a gift. (Psalm 127:4)

The Church is called

* to receive, nurture and treasure children as a gift from God;
* to proclaim the Gospel to children, in ways that empower them to receive and respond to God's love;
* to give high priority to the quality of planning for children and the preparation and support to those who minister with them;
* to include children, in fulfillment of the Baptismal Covenant, as members and full participants in the Eucharistic community and in the church's common life of prayer, witness and service.

Ministry to the Child

Then Jesus took the children in his arms, placed his hands on each of them and blessed them. (Mark 10:16)

The Church is called

* to love, shelter, protect and defend children within its own community and in the world, especially those who are abused, neglected or in danger;
* to nurture and support families in caring for their children, acting in their children's best interest, and recognizing and fostering the children's spirituality and unique gifts;
* to embrace children who seek Christian nurture independently of their parent's participation in the church;

- to advocate for the integrity of childhood and the dignity of all the children at every level of our religious, civic and political structures.

Ministry of the Child

A child shall lead them. (Isaiah 11:6)

The Church is called

- to receive children's special gifts as signs of the Reign of God;
- to foster community beyond the family unit, in which children, youth and adults know each other by name, minister to each other, and are partners together in serving Christ in the world;
- to appreciate children's abilities and readiness to represent Christ and his church, to bear witness to him wherever they may be, and according to gifts given them, to carry on Christ's work of reconciliation in the world, and to take their place in the life, worship, and governance of the church. (*Ministry of the Laity*, BCP p. 855)

THE CHARTER FOR LIFELONG CHRISTIAN FORMATION

The Charter for Lifelong Christian Formation was overwhelmingly adopted at the Episcopal Church's General Convention by Resolution 2009-A082.

Through the Episcopal Church, God *Invites* all people:

- To enter into a prayerful life of worship, continuous learning, intentional outreach, advocacy and service.

- To hear the Word of God through scripture, to honor church teachings, and continually to embrace the joy of Baptism and Eucharist, spreading the Good News of the risen Christ and ministering to all.

- To respond to the needs of our constantly changing communities, as Jesus calls us, in ways that reflect our diversity and cultures as we seek, wonder and discover together.

- To hear what the Spirit is saying to God's people, placing ourselves in the stories of our faith, thereby empowering us to proclaim the Gospel message.

> *You did not choose me, but I chose you and appointed you to go and bear fruit.* (John 15:14–16)

Through the Episcopal Church, God *Inspires* all people:

- To experience Anglican liturgy, which draws us closer to God, helps us discern God's will and encourages us to share our faith journeys.

- To study Scripture, mindful of the context of our societies and cultures, calling us to seek truth anew while remaining fully present in the community of faith.

- To develop new learning experiences, equipping disciples for life in a world of secular challenges and carefully listening for the words of modern sages who embody the teachings of Christ.

- To prepare for a sustainable future by calling the community to become guardians of God's creation.

*I am giving you these commands that you
may love one another.* (John 15:17)

Through The Episcopal Church, God *Transforms* all people:

- By doing the work Jesus Christ calls us to do, living into the reality that we are all created in the image of God and carrying out God's work of reconciliation, love, forgiveness, healing, justice and peace.
- By striving to be a loving and witnessing community, which faithfully confronts the tensions in the church and the world as we struggle to live God's will.
- By seeking out diverse and expansive ways to empower prophetic action, evangelism, advocacy and collaboration in our contemporary global context.
- By holding all accountable to lift every voice in order to reconcile oppressed and oppressor to the love of God in Jesus Christ our Lord.

*Christian Faith Formation in the Episcopal Church is
a lifelong journey with Christ, in Christ, and to Christ.*

THE FIVE MARKS
OF MISSION

The Mission of the Church Is the Mission of Christ

To proclaim the Good News of the Kingdom

To teach, baptize and nurture new believers

To respond to human need by loving service

To seek to transform unjust structures of society, to challenge violence of every kind and to pursue peace and reconciliation

To strive to safeguard the integrity of creation and sustain and renew the life of the earth

The Five Marks of Mission, developed by the Anglican Consultative Council between 1984 and 1990, and adopted by the Episcopal Church's General Convention in 2009, have won wide acceptance among Anglicans, and have given churches and dioceses around the world a practical and memorable "checklist" for mission activities.

WHAT ARE THE MILLENNIUM DEVELOPMENT GOALS?

They're life-saving, world-changing, and, most importantly, doable.

The eight Millennium Development Goals (MDGs) were set by the United Nations in 2000. They're tangible targets to make significant progress in solving the world's most pressing problems by the year 2015. One hundred eighty-nine nations have signed on (including the United States). The MDGs are:

Goal 1: Eradicate extreme poverty and hunger

Goal 2: Achieve universal primary education

Goal 3: Promote gender equality and empower women

Goal 4: Reduce child mortality

Goal 5: Improve maternal health

Goal 6: Combat HIV/AIDS, malaria, and other diseases

Goal 7: Ensure environmental sustainability

Goal 8: Develop a global partnership for development

The Episcopal Church is one of many churches that have made the MDGs a priority. Some parishes are partnering by pledging .07% of their budgets toward funding some of these goals. Episcopalians are also actively lobbying our government to do the same thing. Find out more at *www.globalgood.org*.

DAILY DEVOTIONS FOR INDIVIDUALS AND FAMILIES
(from The Book of Common Prayer, pages 136–140)

These devotions follow the basic structure of the Daily Office of the Church.

When more than one person is present, the Reading and the Collect should be read by one person, and the other parts said in unison, or in some other convenient manner. (For suggestions about reading the Psalms, see page 582 of the BCP.)

For convenience, appropriate Psalms, Readings, and Collects are provided in each service. When desired, however, the Collect of the Day, or any of the Collects appointed in the Daily Offices, may be used instead.

The Psalms and Readings may be replaced by those appointed in

a) the Lectionary for Sundays, Holy Days, the Common of Saints, and Various Occasions, page 888 of the BCP.
b) the Daily Office Lectionary, page 934 of the BCP.
c) some other manual of devotion which provides daily selections for the Church Year.

In the Morning

From Psalm 51

Open my lips, O Lord, *
   and my mouth shall proclaim your praise.
Create in me a clean heart, O God, *
   and renew a right spirit within me.
Cast me not away from your presence *
   and take not your holy Spirit from me.
Give me the joy of your saving help again *
   and sustain me with your bountiful Spirit.
Glory to the Father, and to the Son, and to the Holy Spirit: *
   as it was in the beginning, is now, and will be for ever.
Amen.

A Reading

Blessed be the God and Father of our Lord Jesus Christ! By his great mercy we have been born anew to a living hope through the resurrection of Jesus Christ from the dead. *I Peter 1:3*

A period of silence may follow.

A hymn or canticle may be used; the Apostles' Creed may be said.

Prayers may be offered for ourselves and others.

The Lord's Prayer

The Collect

Lord God, almighty and everlasting Father, you have brought us in safety to this new day: Preserve us with your mighty power, that we may not fall into sin, nor be overcome by adversity; and in all we do, direct us to the fulfilling of your purpose; through Jesus Christ our Lord. *Amen.*

At Noon

From Psalm 113

Give praise, you servants of the LORD; *
    praise the Name of the LORD.
Let the Name of the LORD be blessed, *
    from this time forth for evermore.
From the rising of the sun to its going down *
    let the Name of the LORD be praised.
The LORD is high above all nations, *
    and his glory above the heavens.

A Reading

O God, you will keep in perfect peace those whose minds are fixed on you; for in returning and rest we shall be saved; in quietness and trust shall be our strength. *Isaiah 26:3; 30:15*

Prayers may be offered for ourselves and others.

The Lord's Prayer

The Collect

Blessed Savior, at this hour you hung upon the cross, stretching out your loving arms: Grant that all the peoples of the earth may look to you and be saved; for your mercies' sake. *Amen.*

or this

Lord Jesus Christ, you said to your apostles, "Peace I give to you; my own peace I leave with you:" Regard not our sins, but the faith of your Church, and give to us the peace and unity of that heavenly City, where with the Father and the Holy Spirit you live and reign, now and for ever. *Amen.*

In the Early Evening

This devotion may be used before or after the evening meal.

The Order of Worship for the Evening, page 109, may be used instead.

O gracious Light,
pure brightness of the everliving Father in heaven,
O Jesus Christ, holy and blessed!

Now as we come to the setting of the sun,
and our eyes behold the vesper light,
we sing your praises O God: Father, Son, and Holy Spirit.

You are worthy at all times to be praised by happy voices,
O Son of God, O Giver of life,
and to be glorified through all the worlds.

A Reading

It is not ourselves that we proclaim; we proclaim Christ Jesus as Lord, and ourselves as your servants, for Jesus' sake. For the same God who said, "Out of darkness let light shine," has caused his light to shine within us, to give the light of revelation—the revelation of the glory of God in the face of Jesus Christ. *2 Corinthians 4:5–6*

Prayers may be offered for ourselves and others.

The Lord's Prayer

The Collect

Lord Jesus, stay with us, for evening is at hand and the day is past; be our companion in the way, kindle our hearts, and awaken hope, that we may know you as you are revealed in Scripture and the breaking of bread. Grant this for the sake of your love. *Amen.*

At the Close of Day

Psalm 134

Behold now, bless the LORD, all you servants of the LORD, *
    you that stand by night in the house of the LORD.
Lift up your hands in the holy place and bless the LORD; *
    the LORD who made heaven and earth bless you out of Zion.

A Reading

Lord, you are in the midst of us and we are called by your Name:
Do not forsake us, O Lord our God. *Jeremiah 14:9, 22*

The following may be said

Lord, you now have set your servant free *
    to go in peace as you have promised;
For these eyes of mine have seen the Savior, *
    whom you have prepared for all the world to see:
A Light to enlighten the nations, *
    and the glory of your people Israel.

Prayers for ourselves and others may follow. It is appropriate that prayers of thanksgiving for the blessings of the day, and penitence for our sins, be included.

The Lord's Prayer

The Collect

Visit this place, O Lord, and drive far from it all snares of the enemy; let your holy angels dwell with us to preserve us in peace; and let your blessing be upon us always; through Jesus Christ our Lord. *Amen.*

The almighty and merciful Lord, Father, Son, and Holy Spirit, bless us and keep us. *Amen.*

COMPLINE

The Officiant begins

The Lord Almighty grant us a peaceful night and a perfect end.
Amen.

Officiant Our help is in the Name of the Lord;

People   The maker of heaven and earth.

The Officiant may then say

Let us confess our sins to God.

Silence may be kept.

Officiant and People

Almighty God, our heavenly Father:
We have sinned against you,
through our own fault,
in thought, and word, and deed,
and in what we have left undone.
For the sake of your Son our Lord Jesus Christ,
forgive us all our offenses;
and grant that we may serve you
in newness of life,
to the glory of your Name. Amen.

Officiant

May the Almighty God grant us forgiveness of all our sins, and the
grace and comfort of the Holy Spirit. *Amen.*

The Officiant then says

O God, make speed to save us.

People   O Lord, make haste to help us.

Officiant and People

Glory to the Father, and to the Son, and to the Holy Spirit: as it
was in the beginning, is now, and will be for ever. *Amen.*

Except in Lent, add Alleluia.

One or more of the following Psalms are sung or said. Other suitable selections may be substituted.

Psalm 4 *Cum invocarem*

1 Answer me when I call, O God, defender of my cause; *
> you set me free when I am hard-pressed;
> have mercy on me and hear my prayer.

2 "You mortals, how long will you dishonor my glory; *
> how long will you worship dumb idols
> and run after false gods?"

3 Know that the LORD does wonders for the faithful; *
> when I call upon the LORD, he will hear me.

4 Tremble, then, and do not sin; *
> speak to your heart in silence upon your bed.

5 Offer the appointed sacrifices *
> and put your trust in the LORD.

6 Many are saying,
> "Oh, that we might see better times!" *
> Lift up the light of your countenance upon us, O LORD.

7 You have put gladness in my heart, *
> more than when grain and wine and oil increase.

8 I lie down in peace; at once I fall asleep; *
> for only you, LORD, make me dwell in safety.

Psalm 31 *In te, Domine, speravi*

1 In you, O LORD, have I taken refuge;
> let me never be put to shame: *
> deliver me in your righteousness.

2 Incline your ear to me; *
> make haste to deliver me.

3   Be my strong rock, a castle to keep me safe,
       for you are my crag and my stronghold; *
           for the sake of your Name, lead me and guide me.

4   Take me out of the net that they have secretly set for me, *
       for you are my tower of strength.

5   Into your hands I commend my spirit, *
       for you have redeemed me,
       O LORD, O God of truth.

Psalm 91   *Qui habitat*

1   He who dwells in the shelter of the Most High *
       abides under the shadow of the Almighty.

2   He shall say to the LORD,
   "You are my refuge and my stronghold, *
       my God in whom I put my trust."

3   He shall deliver you from the snare of the hunter *
       and from the deadly pestilence.

4   He shall cover you with his pinions,
   and you shall find refuge under his wings; *
       his faithfulness shall be a shield and buckler.

5   You shall not be afraid of any terror by night, *
       nor of the arrow that flies by day;

6   Of the plague that stalks in the darkness, *
       nor of the sickness that lays waste at mid-day.

7   A thousand shall fall at your side
   and ten thousand at your right hand, *
       but it shall not come near you.

8   Your eyes have only to behold *
       to see the reward of the wicked.

9   Because you have made the LORD your refuge, *
       and the Most High your habitation,

10   There shall no evil happen to you, *
     neither shall any plague come near your dwelling.

11   For he shall give his angels charge over you, *
     to keep you in all your ways.

12   They shall bear you in their hands, *
     lest you dash your foot against a stone.

13   You shall tread upon the lion and adder; *
     you shall trample the young lion and the serpent
       under your feet.

14   Because he is bound to me in love,
     therefore will I deliver him; *
     I will protect him, because he knows my Name.

15   He shall call upon me, and I will answer him; *
     I am with him in trouble;
     I will rescue him and bring him to honor.

16   With long life will I satisfy him, *
     and show him my salvation.

Psalm 134 *Ecce nunc*

1   Behold now, bless the Lord, all you servants of the Lord, *
     you that stand by night in the house of the Lord.

2   Lift up your hands in the holy place and bless the Lord; *
     the Lord who made heaven and earth bless you out of Zion.

At the end of the Psalms is sung or said

Glory to the Father, and to the Son, and to the Holy Spirit: *
     as it was in the beginning, is now, and will be for ever. Amen.

One of the following, or some other suitable passage of Scripture, is read

Lord, you are in the midst of us, and we are called by your Name:
Do not forsake us, O Lord our God. *Jeremiah 14:9, 22*

People   Thanks be to God.

or this

Come to me, all who labor and are heavy-laden, and I will give you rest. Take my yoke upon you, and learn from me; for I am gentle and lowly in heart, and you will find rest for your souls. For my yoke is easy, and my burden is light. *Matthew 11:28–30*

People   Thanks be to God.

or the following

May the God of peace, who brought again from the dead our Lord Jesus, the great shepherd of the sheep, by the blood of the eternal covenant, equip you with everything good that you may do his will, working in you that which is pleasing in his sight, through Jesus Christ, to whom be glory for ever and ever. *Hebrews 13:20–21*

People   Thanks be to God.

or this

Be sober, be watchful. Your adversary the devil prowls around like a roaring lion, seeking someone to devour. Resist him, firm in your faith. *I Peter 5:8–9a*

People   Thanks be to God.

A hymn suitable for the evening may be sung.

Then follows

V. Into your hands, O Lord, I commend my spirit;

R. For you have redeemed me, O Lord, O God of truth.

V. Keep us, O Lord, as the apple of your eye;

R. Hide us under the shadow of your wings.

Lord, have mercy.
Christ, have mercy.
Lord, have mercy.

Officiant and People

Our Father, who art in heaven,	Our Father in heaven,
hallowed be thy Name,	hallowed be your Name,
thy kingdom come,	your kingdom come,

thy will be done,	your will be done,
on earth as it is in heaven.	on earth as in heaven.
Give us this day our daily bread.	Give us today our daily bread.
And forgive us our trespasses,	Forgive us our sins
as we forgive those	as we forgive those
who trespass against us.	who sin against us.
And lead us not into temptation,	Save us from the time of trial,
but deliver us from evil.	and deliver us from evil.

Officiant Lord, hear our prayer;

People And let our cry come to you.

Officiant Let us pray.

The Officiant then says one of the following Collects

Be our light in the darkness, O Lord, and in your great mercy defend us from all perils and dangers of this night; for the love of your only Son, our Savior Jesus Christ. *Amen.*

Be present, O merciful God, and protect us through the hours of this night, so that we who are wearied by the changes and chances of this life may rest in your eternal changelessness; through Jesus Christ our Lord. *Amen.*

Look down, O Lord, from your heavenly throne, and illumine this night with your celestial brightness; that by night as by day your people may glorify your holy Name; through Jesus Christ our Lord. *Amen.*

Visit this place, O Lord, and drive far from it all snares of the enemy; let your holy angels dwell with us to preserve us in peace; and let your blessing be upon us always; through Jesus Christ our Lord. *Amen.*

A Collect for Saturdays

We give you thanks, O God, for revealing your Son Jesus Christ to us by the light of his resurrection: Grant that as we sing your glory at the close of this day, our joy may abound in the morning as we celebrate the Paschal mystery; through Jesus Christ our Lord. *Amen.*

One of the following prayers may be added

Keep watch, dear Lord, with those who work, or watch, or weep this night, and give your angels charge over those who sleep. Tend the sick, Lord Christ; give rest to the weary, bless the dying, soothe the suffering, pity the afflicted, shield the joyous; and all for your love's sake. *Amen.*

or this

O God, your unfailing providence sustains the world we live in and the life we live: Watch over those, both night and day, who work while others sleep, and grant that we may never forget that our common life depends upon each other's toil; through Jesus Christ our Lord. *Amen.*

Silence may be kept, and free intercessions and thanksgivings may be offered.

The service concludes with the Song of Simeon with this Antiphon, which is sung or said by all

Guide us waking, O Lord, and guard us sleeping; that awake we may watch with Christ, and asleep we may rest in peace.

In Easter Season, add   Alleluia, alleluia, alleluia.

Lord, you now have set your servant free *
   to go in peace as you have promised;

For these eyes of mine have seen the Savior, *
   whom you have prepared for all the world to see:

A Light to enlighten the nations, *
   and the glory of your people Israel.

Glory to the Father, and to the Son, and to the Holy Spirit: *
   as it was in the beginning, is now, and will be for ever. Amen.

All repeat the Antiphon

Guide us waking, O Lord, and guard us sleeping; that awake we may watch with Christ, and asleep we may rest in peace.

In Easter Season, add   Alleluia, alleluia, alleluia.

Officiant Let us bless the Lord.

People Thanks be to God.

The Officiant concludes

The almighty and merciful Lord, Father, Son, and Holy Spirit, bless us and keep us. *Amen.*

MUST-HAVES FOR THE CHRISTIAN EDUCATOR'S SHELF

A Bible

The 1979 Book of Common Prayer

A Bible Concordance

Will Our Children Have Faith? 3rd edition by John Westerhoff (New York: Morehouse, 2012).

The Prayer Book Guide to Christian Education 3rd edition edited by Sharon Ely Pearson and Robyn Szoke (New York: Morehouse, 2009).

Fashion Me a People: Curriculum in the Church by Maria Harris (Nashville: Westminster John Knox Press, 1989).

Stages of Faith: The Psychology of Human Development and the Quest for Meaning by James W. Fowler (San Francisco: HarperOne, 1995).

The Courage to Teach: Exploring the Inner Landscape of a Teacher's Life by Parker J. Palmer (San Francisco: Jossey-Bass, 2007).

Leaders Who Last: Sustaining Yourself and Your Ministry by Margaret J. Marcuson (New York: Seabury Books, 2009)